Marketing Country

Promotion as a Tool for Attracting Foreign Investment

FOREIGN

INVESTMENT

ADVISORY

SERVICE

REVISED EDITION

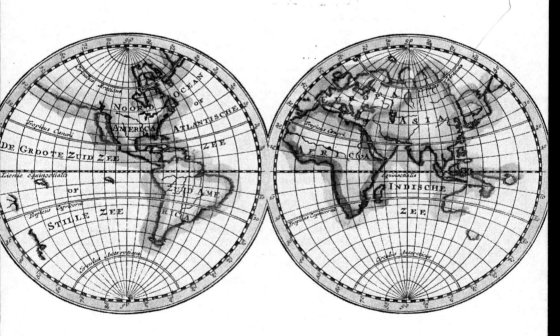

OCCASIONAL

PAPER

13

by
Louis T. Wells, Jr. *and*
Alvin G. Wint

8555819

The International Finance Corporation (IFC), an affiliate of the World Bank, promotes the economic development of its member countries through investment in the private sector. It is the world's largest multilateral organization providing financial assistance directly in the form of loans and equity to private enterprises in developing countries.

The Multilateral Investment Guarantee Agency (MIGA), a new affiliate of the World Bank, encourages equity investment flows to developing countries by offering private investors guarantees against noncommercial, especially political, risks; advising developing member governments on foreign investments; and sponsoring a dialogue between the international business community and host governments on investment issues.

The World Bank is a multilateral development institution whose purpose is to assist its developing member countries further their economic and social progress so that their people may live better and fuller lives.

The findings, interpretations, and conclusions expressed in this publication are those of the authors and do not necessarily represent the views and policies of the International Finance Corporation, or the Multilateral Investment Guarantee Agency, or the World Bank or their Boards of Executive Directors or the countries they represent. The IFC, MIGA, and the World Bank do not guarantee the accuracy of the data included in this publication and accept no responsibility whatsoever for any consequences of their use.

The material in this publication is copyrighted. Request for permission to reproduce portions of it should be sent to the General Manager, Foreign Investment Advisory Service (FIAS), at the address shown in the copyright notice above. FIAS encourages dissemination of its work and will normally give permission promptly and, when the reproduction is for noncommercial purposes, without asking a fee. Permission to copy portions for classroom use is granted through the Copyright Clearance Center, Inc., Suite 910, 222 Rosewood Drive, Danvers, Massachusetts 01923, U.S.A. The backlist of publications by the World Bank and certain of those by its affiliates is shown in the annual Index of Publications, which is available from Distribution Unit, Office of the Publisher, The World Bank, 1818 H Street, N.W., Washington, D.C. 20433, or from Publications, Banque mondiale, 66, avenue d'Iéna, 75116, Paris, France.

Library of Congress Cataloging-in-Publication Data

Wells, Louis T.
     Marketing a country : promotion as a tool for attracting foreign
investment / Louis T. Wells, Jr., Alvin G. Wint. — [Rev. ed.]
        p.   cm. — (FIAS occasional paper ; 13)
     Includes bibliographical references.
     ISBN 0-8213-4659-8
     1. Investments, Foreign. 2. Industrial promotion. I. Wint
Alvin G., 1959– . II. Title. III. Occasional paper (Foreign Investment Advisory
Service) ; 13.
HG4538.W36 2000
332.67'3—dc21

Contents

Foreword to Revised Edition

It has been ten years since the first occasional paper by the Foreign Investment Advisory Service, *Marketing a Country*, was published. In that time *Marketing a Country* has become a standard text on the structure and functions of agencies that promote foreign direct investment. I have seen copies of the paper in ministries and promotion agencies all over the world. Usually pages are dog-eared, and the text is heavily underlined, indicating intense study of the contents.

Marketing a Country created a language for discussing the investment promotion function, and has provided a rationale for successful promotion, especially in developing countries, that has stood the test of time. This edition benefits from an update in an Afterword by one of the original authors, Professor Louis T. Wells, Herbert Johnson Professor of International Business at the Harvard Graduate School of Business. Over the last ten years, Professor Wells has had the opportunity to observe investment promotion in a number of different settings, and uses this experience to review the validity of the main promotion functions identified earlier. He concludes that image building, investor servicing, and investment generation are still important, but that experience also suggests the addition of policy advocacy to the mandate of investment promotion agencies.

Promoting foreign direct investment is just one small part of the larger task of promoting economic development. I am pleased that *Marketing a Country* has made a contribution to both objectives, and expect that this revised edition will enhance that contribution.

Dale R. Weigel
General Manager
Foreign Investment Advisory Service

Acknowledgments

Numerous individuals assisted us in preparing this document and in conducting the research upon which it is based.

We gratefully acknowledge the financial support we received from the World Bank Research Program. Harvard Business School provided additional support for the project. The research project was administered by the Foreign Investment Advisory Service (FIAS) of the International Finance Corporation. We thank Dale K. Weigel, Rafael Benvenisti, Boris Velic, Martin Hartigan, and Joel Bergsman of FIAS for providing helpful comments on various drafts and for assisting us in other ways during this research.

Two colleagues at Harvard Business School, Dennis Encarnation and Benjamin Gomes-Casseres, provided us with valuable comments at various stages during the process of conducting this study and compiling the findings. We also benefited from the comments of two anonymous reviewers of the research proposal.

Of course, this study would not have been possible without the cooperation of many government officials and company managers from several countries. Some of these wish to remain anonymous; in any event we would be unable to mention them all by name. We would, however, like to single out one group of investment promotion officials. We received useful comments from participants in the "Regional Roundtable on Investment Promotion," a seminar sponsored by FIAS and held in Bangkok in October 1988. We are grateful to these officials, and to all those persons who consented to be interviewed for this research.

1

Introduction

This study is about the promotional techniques and structures that countries employ in their competition to attract foreign direct investment. On the basis of the evidence we collected, we argue that:

■ different combinations of promotional techniques are useful at different phases of a promotion program;
■ the type of organization responsible for promotion makes a difference in effectiveness;
■ there are various useful ways to evaluate a promotion program;
■ investment promotion appears to have a statistically significant influence on foreign investment flows; and, particularly important,
■ investment promotion programs have proved effective in attracting only certain kinds of investors.

Promotional techniques consist of providing information to potential investors, creating an attractive image of the country as a place to invest, and providing services to prospective investors. Promotion is only one of several tools available to countries eager to attract foreign investment. Governments offer tax incentives and grants; provide industrial estates, export processing zones, and other infrastructure; and attempt to simplify the bureaucratic procedures facing potential investors, for example. They negotiate bilateral tax, trade, and investment treaties with countries from wherever investments might come. They attempt to create a favorable environment by guaranteeing repatriation of profits, assuring access to imported components, and promising not to expropriate property without compensation. Further, governments recognize the importance of political stability, realistic exchange rates, and rapid growth in attracting foreign investment. Although attracting foreign investment requires efforts in many areas, promotion techniques provide an important mechanism for communicating all these efforts to potential investors.

Promotion efforts are the result of competition by governments in the effort to attract foreign direct investment. This competition is not entirely new; what is new is its aggressiveness and intensity. The new attitudes have, in many instances, led to large expenditures on promotion by governments attempting to attract foreign firms. In 1986 the agencies that we studied spent, on an average, about $8 million on promotion. There has been virtually no research on the effectiveness of these expenditures. Many observers have suspected that much money was wasted. Aggregate data examined in this study, however, showed a significant correlation between promotional programs and the success of countries in attracting foreign investment. Statistical data of this sort encourage one to examine the subject further. More detailed data reported in this study do suggest that certain types of promotion are effective in attracting particular kinds of investors.

For many countries, especially developing countries, the need to do something to attract more foreign direct investment has taken on a new urgency during the 1980s. Between 1979 and 1984, direct investment flows to these countries declined by an annual average rate of 7 percent. During the same period, developing countries suffered from the effects of the debt crisis, which was principally responsible for a 13 percent average annual decline in total bank lending to these countries.[1]

Indeed, growth in the supply of foreign direct investment to both industrial and developing countries slowed during the 1970s and the 1980s. Between 1960 and 1970, foreign direct investment by member countries of the Organization for Economic Cooperation and Development (OECD) grew by an annual average real rate of 11.6 percent; between 1974 and 1979, this rate of growth decreased to 4.9 percent, and during the period 1980–83, it dropped even further, to 3.2 percent.[2]

Given the phenomenon of a potentially declining supply of foreign direct investment, coupled with an increasing or, at best, stable demand for foreign direct investment and limited prospects for receiving development finance from the international banking sector, it is little wonder that competition for foreign direct investment has intensified.[3]

Competition for foreign direct investment has also increased because of the entry of new players. Developing countries that traditionally, because of their large domestic markets or significant reserves of natural resources, did not think it necessary to compete for foreign investment have begun to compete seriously for export-oriented investment. This phenomenon appears to be the result of, among other things, changes in the international economic environment that have characterized the period of the late 1970s and the 1980s. During this period, raw material prices seemed more unstable than usual. At the same time, import-substituting policies seemed to be running out of steam. As a result, an increasing number of developing countries eschewed resource-driven and import-oriented growth strategies in favor of growth strategies that emphasized the export of manufactured goods.[4] Further, during the same period, industrial countries became even more active as they began to court not only firms from other industrial countries but also firms from developing countries that were beginning to spawn their own multinational enterprises.[5]

The new competitive foreign investment environment has prompted analogies between competition among governments for foreign investment and competition among firms for market share.[6] Given the similarities in the nature of the competition, it is not surprising that countries are adopting marketing strategies that parallel those of private companies. Some of the findings of research on company marketing programs can thus benefit countries that are trying to attract investment.

Organizations seeking to develop competitive strategies for marketing activities can, to some extent, manipulate three variables in their overall marketing programs:

- The *product,* or, if the marketer is a country, the intrinsic advantages and disadvantages of the investment site;
- the *price,* or the cost to the investor of locating and operating within the investment site. For governments, this usually means tax incentives, grants, tariff protection, and similar price mechanisms; and
- *promotion,* or activities that disseminate information about, or attempt to create an image of the investment site and provide investment services for the prospective investor.

The focus of this research is on promotion. During the 1980s, many governments either have started investment promotion programs and given those involved the mandate of increasing inward investment or have put pressure on existing promotion agencies to draw in more foreign direct investment.

The Context of the Research

Promotion is, in fact, a part of the wider context of relations between host governments and foreign direct investors. The host governments' side of relations with foreign direct investors consists of a number of steps:

- attracting foreign direct investment through a marketing mix of product, promotional, and pricing strategies;
- screening foreign investment proposals to identify those that are desirable and deserve support;
- monitoring foreign investment to ensure that the investment conforms to expectations; and
- intervening in foreign direct investment if the operations can be made more favorable.

The benefits of foreign investment have long been the subject of debate.[7] Although this research will not add to the debate on the costs and benefits that accrue from foreign direct investment, it will occasionally draw on the conclusions of recent research in this area.[8] Despite the fact that Marxists, nationalists, and dependency-oriented analysts tend to be critical of the role of multinational corporations in developing countries, governments would presumably seek foreign direct investment only if enough officials believed that a substantial portion of this investment was either inherently beneficial to the economy or could be made beneficial through various types of government involvement.

Policies designed to attract investment have various aims:

- to increase the quantity of foreign investment directly;
- to increase the quantity of foreign investment indirectly by, for instance, improving the country's investment image;
- to increase the quality of foreign investment directly or indirectly by targeting specific types of investors; or
- to increase the number of firms competing to invest in a specific project. Research has shown that an increase in the number of firms competing to invest in a project is likely to lead to improvements in the terms and conditions of agreements negotiated by host governments because of the resultant increase in the bargaining power of the host government.[9]

Promotion activities, pricing through investment incentives, and even policies to improve an investment climate may, at times, be considered substitutes in the attraction of investment. Funds for promotion could be used to finance these other activities. As a practical matter, the channeling of funds between promotion and incentives is especially likely in instances in which allocations for investment incentives and investment promotion activities are drawn from the same budget and coordinated by the same government agency.[10] An optimal program to attract foreign investment would allocate resources to each of these marketing activities up to the point at which the marginal return on more resources devoted to each activity would be just less than could be obtained from allocating the resources to other activities that also attract foreign investment. The elements of a marketing mix in a consumer or industrial marketing environment are usually complementary; similarly, in a well-designed program to attract foreign investment, promotion, incentives, and policies designed to improve the "climate" of an investment site should also complement each other. Redesign of part of one element may well affect the working of another part of the marketing program.

We believe that there are phases in a marketing program during which a government can offset increased expenditures on one marketing activity with reduced expenditures on another activity. There may be other phases during which a government must simultaneously increase expenditure on all marketing activities. And there may be still other phases during which governments must follow a certain sequence in devoting resources to the marketing activities of pricing, product, and promotion.

Research has dealt with some of the marketing activities designed to attract investment and some aspects of the relations between governments and foreign investors. Of particular interest have been studies on pricing through investment incentives, and other works on product enhancement strategies, which include studies of the effects of a wide range of economic and political policies.[11] The investment screening function has received some attention;[12] research has been conducted on the function of monitoring foreign investments;[13] and the literature features numerous analyses of the circumstances under which governments tend to intervene in foreign direct investment.[14] Despite the increasing expenditures by countries on investment promotion activities, however, there is almost no research on this subject. The existing literature on international business, economic development, and international marketing provides little in the way of assistance for practitioners in this field. Especially neglected have been the effectiveness of the investment promotion function in general and the relative effectiveness of different promotional techniques and structures.

We feel that extensive research in this area is necessary because of the funds that governments are spending on investment promotion. Further, there is wide disagreement as to whether such expenditures are worthwhile. Statistical analysis of aggregate data, described in detail in chapter 4, suggests that there is a significant relationship between promotion and foreign investment, but analysis based on aggregate figures inevitably remains inconclusive.

This study takes a first step toward remedying the lack of research on investment promotion by analyzing the promotion activities of a number of countries. We shall identify and categorize the promotion strategies that are being used by these governments, analyze the various organizational approaches they employ to carry out the investment promotion function, and develop a framework that will assist in determining which investment promotion techniques and structures are effective and under what conditions.

Objectives of the Research

The problems faced by many governments as they attempt to establish successful investment promotion functions can be categorized into the three broad components of this research project:

- ■ *strategy*—how to identify the combination of the available investment promotion techniques that could be most effectively used to attract investors to their economies;\
- ■ *structure*—how to determine the most appropriate form of organization for the investment promotion function; and
- ■ *performance*—how to evaluate the effectiveness of their investment promotion function, both in general terms, and with respect to specific investment promotion techniques.

Definition of Promotion

For the purposes of this research, investment promotion is defined to include only certain marketing activities through which governments try to attract foreign direct investors. Promotion excludes the granting of incentives to foreign investors, the screening of foreign investment, and negotiation with foreign investors, even though many of the organizations responsible for conducting investment promotion activities may also conduct these other activities.

Investment promotion includes the following types of activity: advertising, direct mailing, investment seminars, investment missions, participation in trade shows and exhibitions, distribution of literature, one-to-one direct marketing efforts, preparation of itineraries for visits of prospective investors, matching prospective investors with local partners, acquiring permits and approvals from various government departments, preparing project proposals, conducting feasibility studies, and providing services to the investor after projects have become operational.

Definition of Investment

The emphasis in this study will be on foreign direct investment: the establishment or purchase by residents of one country of a substantial ownership and management share—usually measured by a minimum equity stake of 10 percent—of a business in another country. At times during the study, reference will be made to reinvestment, defined to include any increase in the foreign holding in an existing investment, either through reinvested earnings or through inflows of new capital. The foreign investor can be either an individual or a corporation, and the investment can be wholly owned by foreigners or a joint venture between foreign and local interests. Foreign direct investment excludes activities such as licensing, subcontracting, and portfolio investment, in which there is either no significant equity or no significant control by foreign management. Nevertheless, promotion efforts may well induce foreign firms to undertake activities other than direct investment. We shall not attempt to track such results.

Conceptual Themes

Two issues studied by others in different contexts have guided this research. The first is that of how to market a product effectively when the buyer is well informed, purchases infrequently, and makes large, discrete purchases. We propose that firms investing abroad go through a decision process that has its analogies in other, more thoroughly studied decisions by corporations to purchase industrial products. The decision processes involved when corporations make large discrete purchases are quite similar to the process by which investment decisions are made. Thus, in this study, we shall draw from the ideas and the research of others who have studied the effectiveness of various approaches to marketing to corporations. This branch of research within industrial marketing suggests that certain promotional techniques are more effective at some stages of the industrial buying decision process than at others. Similar techniques have similar functions in the investment decision process.

The second issue is the choice whether to organize certain nontraditional government activities in the government or in the private sector. Both possibilities, plus some intermediate approaches, seem to exist for investment promotion efforts. Certain activities other than investment promotion are undertaken in some countries by the public sector even though they have many of the same attributes as activities that usually reside in the private sector. In other countries, however, these same activities, while financed by the public sector, are managed by the private sector. The reasons activities reside in the public sector but are sometimes managed by private organizations have been studied by others. In this research we have drawn on these other studies.

Research Design

We used two approaches in conducting this research—statistical analysis and field-based interviews. In order to establish that investment promotion had a significant influence on inflows of foreign investment, we used multiple regression analysis to test data on fifty industrial and developing countries. We divided the set of countries on the basis of their involvement or lack of involvement in investment promotion and included in the regression model other variables researchers have suggested are important determinants of foreign investment. The analysis indicated a strong positive relation between investment promotion and inflows of foreign investment. These tests could not, however, evaluate the effectiveness of particular promotional techniques and structures, and they left serious questions of causality.

Since there has been very little research on the subject of investment promotion, to conduct evaluations of the effectiveness of particular promotional techniques and structures, we had to gather data at first hand in the field.[15] Thus, the second approach that we used was structured interviews with individuals involved directly and indirectly in investment promotion. We interviewed promotional officials from countries that have been active in investment promotion. Since we were not trying to explain why countries engage in investment promotion, we made no attempt to conduct interviews in countries that have not engaged in investment promotion activities.

The interviews were conducted in three phases. Phase 1 consisted of interviews with investment promotion officials from a selection of countries that had investment promotion representatives on the East Coast of the United States. It seemed likely that most countries active in investment promotion would have some investment promotion representation in the primary financial region of the world's largest economy. In this phase, we conducted interviews with promotional representatives (in one case the former director of a promotional program) from twenty countries. These twenty countries were chosen from the thirty countries listed by the *Business Facilities* magazine as those most actively seeking inward investment from U.S.-based companies.[16] We felt that the selection and examination of twenty countries at this stage would provide sufficient data for an appreciation for the general patterns of investment promotion.

These interviews were focused on the countries' involvement in investment promotion; the differing roles of source and host country offices; the promotional techniques and structures used including any changes over time; and the methods used, and success achieved in measuring the effectiveness of various promotional techniques. Promotional representatives were also requested to indicate those countries that they felt were active and successful in investment promotion.

Sample Selection

We used the information obtained from these representatives of promotional operations to choose a sample of countries in which to conduct more intensive, on-site investigations into the investment promotion operation. These investigations composed phase 2 of the research, which consisted of on-site research on the techniques and structures employed by ten investment promotion operations in nine countries and one territory. A carefully selected sample of ten agencies would provide, it seemed, sufficient variation in patterns to cover adequately the spectrum of investment promotion techniques and structures in use.

Several factors were taken into consideration in choosing the ten promotion operations. Countries that, by their own admission, had made unsuccessful promotional efforts in the past but had since begun to promote investment more successfully were included. We felt that if we examined promotional efforts over time in these countries, we would be in a better position to identify the impact of promotion. In such environments, it would be possible at least partially to control the effects of other variables, such as political and economic (product) factors, and incentives (price) factors, that are also involved in the attraction of foreign direct investment.

The criteria for choosing the final list of countries included travel budget considerations, the ability to gain access to promotion agencies, and the inclusion of countries with a reputation for effective promotional efforts. We also included in the sample countries that had changed promotional approaches over time with changes in results. Another objective was that the final sample of countries should include countries at different levels of development, of varying size, and in different locations. At the same time, because of the a priori hypothesis that the type of investment most likely to be influenced by the efforts of promotion agencies was internationally mobile, export-oriented investment, we made an attempt to include more than one country with access, often preferential, to the same regional market. Costa Rica and Jamaica, for example, both had preferential access to the United States market through the Caribbean Basin Initiative; Britain and Ireland both had preferential access to the European Community. In the end, the following locations were chosen for on-site research visits: Britain, Canada, Costa Rica, Indonesia, Ireland, Jamaica, Malaysia, Scotland, Singapore, and Thailand.

These on-site research visits consisted of interviews with promotional officials, other government officials, representatives of the chambers of commerce of the United States and other countries, commercial officers of the U.S. embassy, representatives of foreign aid organizations, representatives of international organizations, and consultants involved in investment promotion. In all, about 100 interviews were conducted during this phase of the research. The interviews attempted to probe more deeply into the promotional techniques and structures identified during the interviews we conducted during the first phase. We made attempts to corroborate information received from promotion agencies through interviews with other more disinterested parties. During this phase, we also conducted archival research to acquire secondary information on past investment promotion techniques and structures and independent evaluations of the investment promotion activities of the promotional operations under study.

During phase 3, we interviewed managers from firms that invested in one or more of the countries under review or were considering such investments. The goal was to measure the effectiveness of various approaches to promotion. We interviewed managers involved in thirty investment decisions from twenty-eight companies. The list of companies was stratified along the dimension of type of investment—that is, whether the investment was for export or to serve the domestic economy. For practical reasons, the focus was on foreign direct investors from the United States. In these interviews we focused on the early stages of the decision process, to determine the effect of promotion methods on the investment decision. This approach was similar to the methodology employed in some of the early studies of the foreign investment decision process.[17] Since an understanding of the decisionmaking process required that managers recall the inputs into this process, the investments we studied were all recent (1985 to 1987).

Aside from obtaining specific information about the motivations behind particular investment decisions and the role of promotion agencies in the making of these decisions, we also used the interviews to obtain more general information about the promotional techniques that foreign investors consider most effective.

Methodologies Used in Related Marketing Research

The most difficult methodological issue in this research has been measurement of the effectiveness of promotion efforts. The problem is similar to that of measuring the effectiveness of advertising and promotion in a consumer or industrial marketing setting. The methodological approaches used in previous studies of advertising effectiveness can be grouped into the following three general categories: factual recall of advertisements, econometric studies, and controlled experiments.[18] One of the debates in the literature on this subject concerns the relevant standard of effectiveness: increases in sales, or increases in an intermediate measure other than final sales. Among the measures that are often advocated as appropriate intermediate measures are attitudinal changes caused by advertising. Those who advocate using an intermediate measure contend that advertising is only one of the factors influencing sales and that it is not sufficiently dominant to be directly related to sales.[19]

Many marketing theorists still maintain, however, that the only appropriate measure of advertising effectiveness is the effect of advertising on sales. This view usually rests on the premise that although there are indeed many factors that affect sales, statistical techniques can be used to distinguish the effect of advertising from that of other factors. Proponents of this school of thought also argue that attitudinal changes, as usually measured, are unreliable indicators of effectiveness, since they can follow sales as well as lead them.[20] They argue further that one cannot rely on the factual recall technique that assumes that factual recall of advertising leads to attitudinal and behavioral changes, which by themselves are an adequate measure of the effectiveness of the advertising, since several studies have suggested that there may be little relation between what a person recalls on the one hand and what he does on the other.[21]

Nevertheless, we relied primarily on intermediate measures of effectiveness for two reasons: Since "sales" actually represented infrequent and important investments in this instance, the sequence of attitude and "sale" could be more easily distinguished than in a consumer marketing setting, and for this study, an attempt was made to elicit "factual recall" of the factors that had influenced a decision process, in addition to "factual recall" of what was seen or heard. We also conducted an econometric study, however, to test for the influence of promotion.

In this research, we drew on studies done by third parties on the effectiveness of various investment promotion techniques. For these evaluations a variety of methodologies was used. In general, the evaluations of advertising and service activities relied upon interviews with managers to assess the success of particular advertising campaigns in their ability to make attitudinal changes or the success of particular service programs in providing the investor with adequate levels of service. The evaluations of promotional activities designed to generate investment directly relied primarily upon attempts to count the number of investments these activities generated in determining how effective the particular promotional activities had been.

Investment promotion agencies themselves use different methodologies to evaluate the effectiveness of their own investment promotion activities. We shall describe the process by which these evaluations are conducted and, where they are available, the results of the evaluations.

Before examining the effectiveness of the promotional efforts of countries, however, we shall address the first two issues that governments face in creating a new investment promotion function or improving an existing one. They need to develop a set of investment promotion strategies. The research findings that will be set out in chapter 2 suggest that in this effort, governments can benefit from viewing investment promotion as a type of industrial marketing. Governments then need to identify the appropriate organizational structure to implement these promotion strategies. The research findings that will be set out in chapter 3 suggest that this organizational choice falls within the realm of public or private management of certain government activities.

Notes

1. These figures are calculated from Table VI-2 "Total Resource Flows to Developing Countries by Major Types of Flow, 1950–1964, in *Twenty-Five Years of Development Cooperation: A Review* (Development Assistance Committee, Organization for Economic Cooperation and Development [OECD] November 1985), 162.

2. See Investment Canada, *Annual Report, 1985-1986.* part I, for a discussion of changes in the international environment of foreign direct investment.

3. See David J. Goldsbrough, Investment Trends and Prospects: The Link with Bank Lending," *in Investing in Development: New Roles for Private Capital?* ed. Theodore H. Moran et al. (Washington, D.C. Overseas Development Council 1986) for a discussion of the potential substitutability of foreign direct investment for bank lending. Goldsbrough forecasts that during the latter half of the 1980s foreign direct investment will increase in certain groups of countries but not sufficiently to compensate for reduced inflows from commercial lending.

4. For a discussion of the way one large, resource-rich country has attempted to shift to an export-oriented growth strategy, see Louis T. Wells, Jr.. and Alvin C. Wint. Indonesia: Choice of Industrialization Strategy." HBS note no. N9-387-099, 1987.

5. For a discussion of the new multinationals that are being spawned in the Third World, see LouisT. Wells, Jr., *Third World Multinationals: The Rise of Foreign Investment from Developing Countries* (Cambridge. MA: MIT Press. 1963); and Sanjaya Lall, *The New Multinationals: The Spread of Third World Enterprises* (New York: Institute for Research and Information on Multinationals, John Wiley and Sons. 1983). An example of this phenomenon is that, in 1987, Ireland had promotional offices in Hong Kong and Korea; the Netherlands, in Taiwan. Mauritius had sent missions to Hong Kong to persuade Hong Kong garment makers to establish factories in Mauritius.

6. See, for example, Dennis *J.* Encarnation and Louis T. Wells, Jr., "Competitive Strategies in Global Industries: A view from Host Governments," in *Competition in Global Industries,* ed. Michael E. Porter (Boston: Harvard Business School Press, 1986).

7. For a summary of the debate in the international business literature, see Alvin G. Wint, "Subfield Paper on International Business-Government Relations" (Boston: Harvard Business School, December 1986).

8. See Dennis J. Encarnation and l.ouis T. Wells, Jr., "Evaluating Foreign Investment," *Investing in Development,* ed. Moran et al., chap. 2.

9. Research conducted within the framework of bargaining powsr models has swamped the literature on international business-governmant relations. Some of the earliest of these studies were Raymond Vernon, "Long-Run Trends in Concession Contract," *Proceedings of the American Society for International Law* (April 1967); and Louis T. Wells, Jr., "The Evolution of Concession Agreements in Underdeveloped Countries" (Boston: Harvard Development Advisory Service, March 1971). For research dealing specifically with the effect of increasing competition among firms on the bargaining power of the host government, see Joseph M. Grieco, "Between Dependence and Autonomy: India's Experience with the International Computer Industry," *International Organization* 36 (Summer 1982): 609–32.

10. See Stephen Guisinger, "Host-Country Policies to Attract and Control Foreign Investment," in *Investing in Development,* ed. Moran et al., p. 163.

11. Important studies of investment incentives indude Grant Reuber et al., *Private Foreign Investment in Development* (Oxford: Clarendon Press, 1973); and, more recently, Stephen E. Guisinger and associates, *Investment Incentives and Performance Requirements* (New York: Praeger Publishers, 1985). The economic development and international business literature is filled with suggestions about what countries should do to improve their investment cli-

mates. For a primer, seee Reuber et al., *Private Foreign Investment;* Sanjaya Lall and Paul Streeten, *Foreign Investment, Transnationals, and Developing Countries* (Boulder, Colorado: Westview Press, 1977); and Richard D. Robinson, *Foreign Investment in the Third World: A Comparative Study of Selecteal Developing Country Investment Promotion Programs* (Washington, D.C.: Chamber of Commerce of the United States, 1980).

12. See, for example, Dennis J. Encarnation and Louis T. Wells, "Sovereignty en Garde: Negotiating with Foreign Investors," *International Organization* 39 (Winter 1985): 47–78.

13. See, for example, J. de la Torre, "Foreign Investment and Economic Development: Conflict and Negotiation," *Journal of International Business Studies,* Fall 1981.

14. See, for example, Thomas Poynter, "Government Intervention in LDCs: The Experience of MNCs," *Journal of International Business Studies,* Spring/Summer 1982; Stephen J. Kobrin, "Foreign Enterprise and Forced Divestment in LDCs," *International Organization,* Winter 1980; David Bradley, "Managing against Expropriation," *Harvard Business Review,* July–August 1977; Yves L Doz and C. K. Prahalad, "How MNCs Cope with Host Government Intervention; *Harvard Business Review,* March–April 1980; and Dennis J. Encarnation and Sushil Vachani, "Foreign Ownership: When Hosts Change the Rules," *Harvard Business Review,* September–October 1985.

15. For a discussion of the appropriate research designs corresponding to different research problems, see Thomas Bonoma, "Case Research in Marketing: Opportunities, Problems, and a Process," *Journal of Marketing Research* 12 (May 1985).

16. See *Business Facilities* 20 (no.3, March 1987): 38–50.

17. See, for example, Yair Aharoni, *The Foreign Investment Decision Process* (Boston, MA: Division of Research, Harvard Business School 1966); and Raghbir S. Basi, *Determinants of United States Private Direct Investments in Foreign Countries* (Kent, Ohio: Kent State University Press, 1963).

18. For an interesting review of the state of the art in copy testing and factual recall as methods of measuring the effectiveness of advertising, see Devid W. Stewart, Connie Pechmann, Srinivasan Ratneshwar, Jon Stroud, and Beverly Bryant, "Methodological and Theoretical Foundations of Advertising Copytesting: A Review," *Current Issues and Research in Advertising* 2 (1985): 1–74.

19. An early proponent of this view was Russell H. Colley; see his *Defining Advertising Goals for Measured Advertising Results* (New York: Association of National Advertisers, 1961); see also Russell Colley, "Squeezing the Waste out of Advertising," *Harvard Business Review*, September–October 1962, 76–88.

20. This view is presented by Nariman K. Dhalla, "How to Set Advertising Budgets," *Journal of Advertising Research* 17 (no. 5, October 1977): 14.

21. For a discussion of several of these studies, see Jack B. Haskins, "Factual Recall as a Measure of Advertising Effectiveness," *Journal of Advertising Research*, March 1964, 2–28.

2

The Roles of Various Promotion
Techniques

Conventional wisdom holds that a targeted strategy is the most appropriate approach to investment promotion.[1] A study of investment promotion made by SRI International posits that "there is almost universal consensus on the point that investment promotion activities should be targeted, both in order to direct investment flows into 'priority' sectors and to utilize scarce promotional resources efficiently."[2] There is a certain amount of logic to support this conclusion. Empirical observations, however, suggest that, contrary to conventional recommendations, some promotion agencies adopt a general approach to promotion and others use a mix of techniques that include targeted and general techniques. The frequency with which techniques other than targeted approaches appear makes one wonder whether targeted promotional strategies are more effective than general strategies under all conditions. If not, under what conditions are other approaches more effective?

In this chapter we shall propose a model that is consistent with the approaches to the investment promotion processes that we observed. Under this model targeted promotional techniques and

20

general promotional techniques are likely to be used, and to be effective, in different circumstances. This model explicitly recognizes the close parallels between the industrial buying and the investment decisions and, accordingly, draws on the work of researchers who have studied the promotional techniques that are most effective in selling industrial products to corporations.

Types of Investment Promotion Techniques

Although investment promotion is ultimately aimed at attracting investors, at another level of generalization promotion activities are designed to accomplish three different objectives:

- to improve a country's image within the investment community as a favorable location for investment (image-building activities);
- to generate investment directly (investment-generating activities); and
- to provide services to prospective and current investors (investment-service activities).

Image-building and investment-service activities have as their ultimate objectives the attraction of more investment. But their immediate goals are different, and, it could be argued, appropriate measures of effectiveness are different.

In the course of interviews with officials from promotion agencies we identified at least twelve different promotional techniques that were in use by at least some of the countries that we studied, as follows:

1. Advertising in general financial media.
2. Participating in investment exhibitions.
3. Advertising in industry- or sector-specific media.
4. Conducting general investment missions from source country to host country or from host country to source country.

5. Conducting general information seminars on investment opportunities.
6. Engaging in direct mail or telemarketing campaigns.
7. Conducting industry- or sector-specific investment missions from source country to host country or vice versa.
8. Conducting industry- or sector-specific information seminars.
9. Engaging in firm-specific research followed by "sales" presentations.
10. Providing investment counseling services.
11. Expediting the processing of applications and permits.
12. Providing postinvestment services.

These promotional techniques were typically employed for different purposes. Some, especially techniques 1 to 5, were usually directed toward building a particular image for the country; in contrast, techniques 6 to 9 were used to generate investment directly, and techniques 10 to 12 were investment-service techniques. Although the goals of the techniques overlapped to some extent, this classification scheme seems to capture reasonably well the objectives that typically lay behind the use of the various techniques.

Image-Building Techniques

All promotion agencies in the sample were using, or had used in the past, one or more of the image-building techniques (see table 1).

Most agencies used image-building techniques simply with the objective of changing the image of the country as a place to invest. These countries had no expectation that these activities would generate investment directly. Britain's IBB, Investment Canada, Ireland's IDA, Singapore's EDB, Locate in Scotland, and Malaysia's MIDA all fell into this category. Shortly after their creation, the IBB and Investment Canada engaged in intense promotional campaigns, with the intention of changing the image of their respective countries in the corporate investment communities. IDA began its active promotional activities with an advertising campaign designed to

Table 1. Primary Image-Building Techniques Used by Agencies

Locality	Promotion agency	Image-building techniques used
Britain	Invest in Britain Bureau (IBB)	1,2,4,5
Canada	Investment Canada	1,3
Costa Rica	Costa Rican Investment Promotion Program (CINDE)	2,3,4
Indonesia	Investment Coordinating Board (BKPM)	4,5
Ireland	Industrial Development Authority (IDA)	1,3
Jamaica	Jamaica National Investment Promotion (JNIP)	2,3,4,5
Malaysia	Malaysian Industrial Development Authority (MIDA)	2,4
Scotland	Locate in Scotland (LIS)	1,2
Singapore	Economic Development Board (EDB)	1
Thailand	Board of Investment (BOI)	1

establish an image of Ireland as a prime site for internationally mobile investment. The EDB advertised in the wake of the recession of the mid-1980s with the aim of reminding the business community that Singapore was, despite the recent recession, still a very attractive investment location. MIDA and Locate in Scotland maintained a minimal advertising exposure in media aimed at particular industrial sectors to keep their respective countries in the minds of potential investors.

Another, smaller group of agencies expected image-building techniques to generate investment directly but were disappointed that the activities were not effective in accomplishing their goals. The early years of Jamaica's JNIP and of Costa Rica's CINDE and the efforts of Indonesia's BKPM illustrate this second group of agencies. During the early years of its life, Jamaica's JNIP used advertising, missions, and seminars and participated in investment exhibitions in an attempt to create a favorable image in the international investment community following the election of the conservative Seaga government. The agency also, however, expected that these techniques would lead directly to investments from abroad. Eventually, JNIP's disappointment led it to change its approach to promotion. CINDE began investment promotion efforts by using promotional activities such as seminars, participation in investment exhibitions, and missions, all designed to generate investment directly. Although CINDE, in 1987, still participated in investment exhibitions, the agency no longer expected these exhibitions to produce investment directly. It had, moreover, shifted its principal focus to other approaches. Indonesia's BKPM used investment missions and seminars, arranged either by the agency or by consultants, as the agency's primary promotional techniques. BKPM expected that these events would lead directly to investments, although we believe that they were not effective in that effort.

One agency in the sample fit into a third category: Thailand's BOI expected image-building techniques to generate investment directly and found that the techniques did indeed seem to generate investment. The agency sponsored a promotional campaign in Japan during 1986 that relied principally on advertising and direct mail activities. The campaign appeared to be successful in generating investment directly. We believe, however, that this case represents an exception to the general pattern.[3]

Investment-Generating Techniques

We classified direct mail or telemarketing campaigns (technique 6), industry or sector-specific investment missions and information seminars (techniques 7-8), and firm-specific research leading to "sales" presentations (technique 9) as investment-generating. The use of these techniques by the various agencies we studied is listed in table 2.

All the agencies in the study that had used investment-generating techniques considered that these techniques could generate investment directly. (Only Indonesia's BKPM had not, before 1988, used any investment-generating techniques.) The consensus among agencies, however, was that these techniques were effective only to the extent that they were a vehicle through which decisionmakers, in companies likely to invest, could be identified, personally contacted, and encouraged to invest in a particular coun-

Table 2. Primary Investment-Generating Techniques Used by Agencies

Locality	Promotion agency	Investment-generating techniques used
Britain	Invest in Britain Bureau (IBB)	6,9
Canada	Investment Canada	9
Costa Rica	Costa Rican Investment Promotion Program (CINDE)	6,9
Ireland	Industrial Development Authority (IDA)	9
Jamaica	Jamaica National Investment Promotion (JNIP)	6, 8
Malaysia	Malaysian Industrial Development Authority (MIDA)	6
Scotland	Locate in Scotland (LIS)	6,9
Singapore	Economic Development Board (EDB)	9
Thailand	Board of Investment (BOI)	7

try. Jamaica's JNIP, Malaysia's MIDA, and Britain's IBB attempted to identify companies to which tailored presentations could be given primarily by following up direct mail, telemarketing efforts, leads from specific seminars, or, in the case of the IBB, companies in the agency's key corporate directory. Ireland's IDA, Scotland's LIS, Investment Canada, Costa Rica's CINDE, and Singapore's EDB identified prospective companies primarily by engaging in detailed, firm-specific research. The identification of prospective companies was followed by efforts to gain audiences with decisionmakers in these companies so that sales presentations could be conducted.

Investment-Service Techniques

All the investment promotion agencies in the sample regarded investment services such as investment counseling, expediting the processing of applications and permits, and providing postinvestment services (techniques 10-12) as integral components of the investment promotion function. All agencies participated in one or more of these activities. There is, however, no evidence that these activities can serve to generate new investment interest or be a primary force in building or changing images, nor do agencies expect such results. Rather, agencies expect investment-service activities to hold already interested investors, to help keep investors that have already made commitments to invest, and to induce firms to reinvest rather than move to new investment sites.

There appears to be little doubt, on the basis of our observations of the different objectives and varied activities of agencies, that agencies engage in these three distinct types of promotional activity to accomplish their broader goal of attracting foreign direct investment. Indeed, the extent to which agencies used one type of promotional activity in preference to the other two often seemed to follow a certain sequence and correspond to a particular promotional strategy. We do not believe that the sequence we observed is necessarily right in all circumstances for all countries; we do, however, believe that there is a logic underlying the sequence that can be helpful to countries that are trying to design an appropriate mix of activities.

Strategies of Investment Promotion Programs

Governments tend to engage in all three types of investment promotion activities to varying degrees most of the time, but in their attempts to promote their countries as investment sites, they tend to concentrate their mix of promotional activities at any one time toward image building or investment generation. Thus we were able to classify the investment promotion program of a country, according to its focus at a particular time, as image building or investment generation.

One factor that influenced the mix of promotional techniques used by an agency was its development cycle. In several instances, when government policy was changed to encourage foreign investment, the promotional organization focused on image building with the objective of advising the investment community about the government's new attitude toward foreign investment and its interest in attracting investors. In other instances this concentration on image-building activities coincided with the creation of an agency whose principal function was to attract investment. When the government managers from these organizations felt that an appropriate image had been formed in the minds of prospective investors, the focus of the promotional program shifted to investment generation.

The sequence just described was not followed by all agencies. Several agencies did not begin investment promotion operations by focusing on image building. Others did begin with such a focus, shifted thereafter to a focus on investment generation, but then continued to use image-building activities extensively as changing economic conditions within the country or in the external environment created a new need to change or build images.

By the same reasoning, one can readily conceive of situations in which an agency may have no need to begin its promotional program with a focus on image building. If a country does not have a negative image as a potential site for inward investment, for instance, and if its strengths as such a site are already well known in the international investment community, then there will be substantially less need for the investment promotion agency to develop a promotional strategy that features an initial period of image-building activity. Nevertheless, for many countries the sequence of image building followed by investment-generating activities was frequently observed.

It could be argued that the logic of the patterns we observed is no more than that of a learning process. Countries begin their promotion efforts with an easy technique, such as advertising or conducting a general mission. When they learn that it does not generate investment, they heed the common advice of targeting. While there is evidence that some agencies moved from a focus on image building to a focus on investment generation as their organizations learned more about investment promotion, there is also considerable evidence against this interpretation as an adequate description of the general pattern observed. This evidence comes primarily in the form of country experiences. There is also, however, a literature in industrial marketing that suggests the exist-

ence of and the logic for a promotional strategy such as that identified in this research. The parallels are quite close.

Promotional Strategies in Industrial Marketing

The foreign investment decision is similar in several respects to the
industrial buying decision. In both situations the relevant market
comprises discrete, lumpy, relatively infrequent but often important "purchases" by corporations. This similarity suggests that much
can be understood about the process by which corporations make
investment decisions by examining the work of researchers in industrial marketing on the subject of the way corporations decide
to make industrial purchases.

Researchers have divided the types of purchases industrial buyers make into three groups. Two of these groups are of primary
interest for this study. These are the "first purchase" from a vendor, and the "routine reorder" from the vendor who supplied the
first purchase.[4] For this study, the most relevant section of the
marketing literature is that which explains how corporations make
their first purchases of an industrial product.

To explain the process by which corporations and institutions
make decisions on their first purchases of industrial products, researchers in industrial marketing applied a model that was originally
formulated to describe the process by which innovations are adopted.
This model suggests that buying units in corporations or institutions go through the following five stages when making a first purchase decision: awareness, interest, evaluation, trial, and adoption.[5]

This model of an industrial buying decision was used by marketing researchers to investigate the functions of various information sources at these discrete stages of the purchase or adoption
process. They found that different information sources were most
effective at different stages. During the awareness and the interest
stages, the most effective information sources were impersonal
sources such as advertising. During the evaluation, trial, and adoption stages, however, the most effective information sources in

gaining adoption of the innovation or purchase of the industrial product were personal sources, such as direct contact from salesmen or from other firms.[6]

Reinvestment decisions also have their parallel in industrial marketing. Recall that industrial buying decisions were divided into three groups, one of which was "routine reorder," by which the industrial buyer simply reordered from the vendor that supplied the first purchase.[7] Whereas first purchase decisions present the marketer with the greatest challenge because of the need to outperform the competition to gain the order, for a "routine reorder" the buyer automatically reorders as long as the marketer has maintained adequate levels of quality and service.

On the basis of the existence of stages in industrial buying decisions and the parallels between industrial buying and investment decisions, we argue that a corporation also goes through stages in deciding to make an investment decision. Further, we suggest that promotion agencies design their programs to match the decision processes of their customers. Thus, a promotion agency that has had little involvement or success in attracting companies is likely to be dealing mainly with investors who are in the awareness stage of the investment decision process. Such an agency is likely to use the impersonal promotional techniques that research suggests are most effective at that stage of the industrial buying decision. Agencies that have a record of attracting foreign investors and that come from countries that have sound investment images are likely to be dealing mainly with investors in the evaluation and adoption stages of investment decisions. These agencies are likely to use the personal promotional techniques that research suggests are effective at these stages of the buying decision process. Finally, in countries in which most investment comes from reinvestment by existing firms, and in which this investment nearly satisfies the countries' foreign investment requirements, promotion agencies are likely to deemphasize the function of providing information to new firms, concentrating instead on providing adequate levels of service to existing firms.

Since no agency will, at any particular time, be dealing with investors who are all at the same stage of the investment decision process, every agency can be expected to use all three types of promotional activity. One would expect the pattern that we observed, however, as agencies vary their mix of promotional activities according to the stages at which most prospective investors are in the investment decision process.

The relations among the stages of an industrial buying decision, the stages of an investment decision, and the mix of promotional activities employed by an agency are depicted in table 3.

There are other references in the industrial marketing literature that support the idea of adapting promotional programs to the decision process of the customer. For instance, the classic message that has been used in industrial marketing circles to indicate the importance of the creation by the marketer of an appropriate image and credibility before he makes any efforts to contact prospective buyers directly is McGraw-Hill's "Man-in-Chair" advertisement[8] which appeared in several business magazines. A man sitting in a chair says:

"I don't know who you are.
I don't know your company.
I don't know your company's product.
I don't know what your company stands for.
I don't know your company's customers.
I don't know your company's record.
I don't know your company's reputation.
Now—what was it you wanted to sell me?"
Moral: Sales start *before* your salesman calls—
with business publication advertising.

Country and investment can readily be substituted for company and product in this advertisement, and it provides an illustration in support of the investment promotion strategy that calls for, under certain assumptions, a focus on image building to precede a focus on investment generation.

Table 3. Relationship among Industrial Buying Decisions, Investment Decisions, and an Investment Promotion Program

Buyclass[a]	Information sources[b]	Stages in industrial buying decisions[b]	Stages of investment decisions	Focus of investment promotion
First	Impersonal sources	Awareness	Awareness	Image building
	Advertising	Interest	Interest	
Purchase	Personal sources	Evaluation	Evaluation	Investment generation
		Trial	Trial	
	Other firms salesmen users	Adoption	Adoption	
Routine reorder	Limited information requirements		Implementation	Investment service

a. Typology created by Patrick J. Robinson, Charles W. Faris, and Yoram Wind; see their *Industrial Buying and Creative Marketing* (Boston: Allyn & Bacon, 1967).

b. Derived from Urban B. Ozanne and Gilbert A. Churchill, Jr., "Adoption Research: Information Sources in the Industrial Purchase decision," In *Marketing and the New Science of Planning*, ed. Robert L. King (Chicago: American Marketing Association, series 28, 1968); Ozanne and Churchill "Five Dimensions of the Industrial Adoption Process," *Journal of Marketing* 3(1968): 7-13; Everett M. Rodgers, *Diffusion of Innovations of Marketing* (New York: The Free Press, 1962); and Everett M. Rodgers and F. Floyd Shoemaker, *Communication of Innovation: A Cross-Cultural Approach* (New York: The Free Press, 1971.)

Evidence in support of this promotional strategy is found not only in the industrial marketing literature but also in the experiences of the promotion agencies that were studied during this research.

Empirical Evidence on the Promotional Strategies of Agencies

In testing the empirical validity of the promotional strategy by which an agency attempts to build an image before seeking to generate investment, one would expect to see changes in the mix of promotional activities employed by a particular agency over time.

To support the logic proposed for this strategy, one would further expect to see these changes coupled with changes in the objectives of agencies, or with their success or lack of success, in building images and generating investment.

The empirical test we conducted was for indications of a shift from a focus on image building to a focus on investment generation. This test was conducted for all the agencies that were studied. We sought to ascertain not only whether there was a change in focus, but also the reasons for these changes when they occurred. The results are recorded in table 4.

Six of the agencies that we studied exhibited the expected pattern by starting investment promotion operations with a focus on image building. then shifting to a focus on investment generation.

Table 4. Changes in the Focus of Investment Promotion Programs

Promotion agency	Present focus	Past focus
Invest in Britain Bureau (IBB)	Investment generation	Image building
Investment Canada	Investment generation	Image building
Costa Rican Investment Promotion Program (CINDE)	Investment generation	Image building
Indonesian Investment Coordinating Board (BKPM)	Image building	
Irish Industrial Development Authority (IDA)	Investment generation	Image building
Jamaica National Investment Promotion (JNIP) .	Investment generation	Image building
Malaysian Industrial Development Authority (MIDA)	Investment generation	+
Locate in Scotland (LIS)	Investment generation	+
Singapore Economic Development Board (EDB)	Investment generation	+
Thailand Board of Investment (sot)	Investment generation	Image building

  * Agency started with an image-building stage and has not yet shifted to a focus on investment-generating activities.

  + No evidence was obtained to suggest that the agency started by focusing on image-building activities.

Three of these agencies, Investment Canada, Britain's IBB, and Ireland's IDA, also verified the logic we ascribed to this pattern, since they started investment promotion operations with a focus on image building because of their stated intention to change the image of their respective countries as sites for foreign direct investment.

Canada. In the case of Canada, the program of foreign investment promotion in 1987 was relatively new. Until 1985, the only government agency that dealt with foreign investors was the Foreign Investment Review Agency (FIRA), an agency established during the early 1970s to monitor inward investment. Although FIRA was at some points during its history involved in promoting foreign investment, its primary function was, as its name suggests, to review foreign investment applications and weed out proposals inimical to Canada's well-being.

In 1985 a conservative government came to power on several platforms, including the need to open the economy to foreign investment in order to supply Canada's capital requirements. It was felt that the country's image as a prime location for foreign investment had suffered during the FIRA years, so steps were immediately taken to restore Canada's investment image. The review-oriented FIRA was converted to the promotion-oriented Investment Canada under the auspices of the Investment Canada Act, proclaimed on June 30, 1985, and the first important piece of legislation adopted by the new government. It can be argued that the conversion of FIRA to Investment Canada alone was an image-building activity. Investment Canada's first annual report stated the need to change Canada's investment image: "Canada has always had much to offer investors, but inside and outside the country its business climate was perceived as being unfavorable to investment. Creating a positive perception of Canada as a place to do business and as a preferred location for investment was, therefore, Investment Canada's priority during its first nine months of operation."[9]

To this end, Investment Canada appropriated, during its first year of operation, Can\$3 million from a special Industrial Development Program Fund for the explicit purpose of changing the country's image within the international investment community. This amount, in addition to monies from the regular Investment Canada budget, was used to take out seventy-three double-page advertisements in twenty leading business publications, primarily general financial media, in the United States, the United Kingdom, France, the Federal Republic of Germany, Japan, and Hong Kong. The image-building exercise also included about ninety speeches by ministers and senior officials, eleven articles in Canadian and foreign publications, three audiovisual presentations, and two information booths, as well as press releases and press conferences.

By the agency's second year of operation, the officials concerned felt that the awareness campaign had been successful, and there was a clear shift in the focus of attempts to generate investment. The investment-generating program featured a direct marketing campaign that relied principally on detailed firm-specific research by the research department. Using annual reports and 10-Ks and by tapping into a variety of corporate databases, the agency collected material about companies that might benefit most from the competitive advantages Canada had to offer. The names of corporate prospects were then given either to the consulates or to one of the six investment counselors that were placed in Canadian embassies around the world during 1986–87.

Ireland. The IDA began active promotion during 1969–70, at the time when the organization was changed from a government agency to a quasi-government agency. The agency began its active promotional efforts with an awareness campaign. During 1969–70, the agency spent £IR186,000 on advertising in ten countries. In 1970–71, an intensive advertising campaign was launched in Britain and America in such publications as the *Financial Times, Management Today, The Accountant,* and *The Director.* The campaign was based on the fifteen-year tax holiday theme. The IDA's 1970–71 annual report noted that "The U.S. and British advertisements were aimed at presenting Ireland as a country with a modern industrial economy and correcting outmoded impressions of Ireland."[10]

The transition from image building to investment generation was less sharply defined in the case of the IDA than with Investment Canada, because the agency continued to use image-building activities prominently for the next two decades. IDA's rationale for continuing its advertising program throughout almost two decades is what it perceived as a continuous need to be recognized as a credible player in international investment circles. The IDA has never perceived advertising as effective in generating investment but has seen it rather as a useful technique to create credibility.

In time, IDA pursued different advertising themes as it became necessary, with the development of the country, to change old images and build new ones. When the IDA started promoting investment during the early 1970s, Ireland, for a Western European country, was relatively backward, with an image as an agricultural, picturesque country with limited industrial infrastructure. The IDA used incentives to compensate firms for locating in a "backward" state, but then developed an advertising theme around the fact that Ireland, after its entry into the EC in 1973, provided low-cost access to the EC market. During the late 1970s, the IDA continued basing its advertising message on low-cost manufacture, stressing that American investments in Ireland were more profitable than American investments anywhere else in the world.

By the early 1980s, however, the IDA realized that it could not compete for internationally mobile investment on a cost basis. The country's labor had become more expensive by international standards, and investments in education had significantly improved the skill level of the labor force. Yet independent research conducted for the IDA in 1982 suggested that investors still saw Ireland as a source of low-cost, low-skilled labor. The agency felt that there was a need for a new advertising program to correct the misperceptions of investors and create a new image of Ireland as a source of high-quality labor.

The advertising campaign built upon the increased skill level of the Irish, but also upon two other factors: one was the fact that Ireland alone in Europe had a young, growing labor force, the other, that Ireland was a part of Europe and thus offered access to a market significantly larger than the 3.5 million people within its shores. These three subthemes—skills, youth, and European identity—were combined into the general advertising theme of "We're the Young Europeans," with subtitles about the aptitude and skill level of the labor force.

Britain. The IBB, although created in 1977, did not have the mandate to attract internationally mobile investment to all areas of the United Kingdom until 1980, in the aftermath of the election of the Thatcher government. The organization started investment promotion operations with advertising campaigns. IBB officials perceived that there was a credibility problem, with foreign investors expressing concern about the high levels of labor unrest, frequent power shortages, rising unemployment, and the proliferation of unprofitable state-owned enterprises that had characterized the British economy of the 1970s. As the Thatcher government tried to turn the British economy around, the IBB used testimonial advertising to advise the international business community that Britain wanted inward investment and that such investment was once again profitable in Britain. During the period 1980–82, the amount spent on advertising by the IBB was much greater than that spent during the mid and late 1980s.

The principal indicator of a transition from a focus on image-building activities to a focus on investment-generating activities appeared in 1982. During that year, IBB staff began the development of a key corporate directory. The agency included in this directory any U.S. company with a turnover of at least $50 million and any high-technology company with a minimum turnover of $20 million. Initially 12,000 companies were identified. Companies that already had investments in Britain were excluded, and the database eventually became 5,000 companies. This list of companies was sent to the British consulates and embassies abroad so that consular officials could begin the process of actively generating investment from these corporations.

The transition from image building to investment generation in the case of Britain is less sharply defined than in the case of Canada, because in 1985 the IBB initiated another awareness campaign called "Britain Means Business" (BMB). The impetus for this campaign came from British fears of increased competition from other EC countries, for the IBB thought that misperceptions about the British investment climate persisted within international investment circles. The IBB's 1984 Annual Report states: "BMB will be the first fully-coordinated effort, involving both the public and the private sectors, to promote a united U.K. image overseas."[11] The campaign was to include sixteen seminars, a corporate advertising program, the production of a quarterly magazine *Briefing on Britain* to be mailed to selected companies, a number of receptions, lunches, and dinners for selected executives, and an increased number of visits by U.S. journalists to Britain.

Others. The other three agencies that began investment promotion operations with a focus on image-building activities, then moved to a focus on investment-generating activities—Thailand's BOI, Costa Rica's CINDE, and Jamaica's JNIP—provide some evidence for the alternative proposition, that agencies focus on image-building activities because they are not aware of more effective promotional techniques.

The operations of the Thai BOI show a deliberate transition from a focus on image building to a focus on investment generation, even though the image-building stage was not thought of as such by BOI officials. The BOI had been sporadically promoting investment since about 1980. Activities included participating in general investment missions and seminars and passively reacting to inquiries from prospective investors. The lack of success of image-building techniques in generating investment led to the change to an active investment-generating stage. The transition occurred with the decision to subcontract investment-generating activities in the United States to a consulting company, Arthur D. little, Inc.

The primary promotional technique the consultants relied upon was a series of specific investment missions in the electronics, light manufacturing, and agribusiness sectors. After the consultant's contract with the BOI (and USAID) expired, the BOI continued sponsoring specific investment missions; a mission was conducted in the jewelry sector, for example, in conjunction with the U.S. Chamber of Commerce in Thailand. All these missions were organized with the objective of generating investment directly.

In the case of Costa Rica, image-building techniques characterized CINDE's early years after the creation of the agency in 1982, but, as in the case of Thailand, these were image building in practice, but not by design. The agency began its investment promotion efforts by conducting missions to the United States, holding seminars, and participating in investment exhibitions. These activities were conducted with the intention of generating investment, however, not of building an image. The CINDE officials were disappointed that their activities did not succeed in generating investment. No studies have been carried out to ascertain whether they were effective in building CINDE'S image as a player in the inward investment game in selected sectors such as textiles.

For CINDE the transition to an investment-generating stage was deliberate and planned, coinciding with the receipt of consulting advice from Ireland's IDA. During 1984–85 the agency set up an investment-generating campaign, the principal pillar of which was a direct marketing program that involved cold calls to a targeted group of companies in the United States by CINDE's overseas representatives. These calls were followed with well-researched sales presentations.

Jamaica's JNIP was the other agency that started investment promotion operations in an image-building stage, at least in part, it seems, because of the agency's lack of experience in investment promotion. The JNIP was created in 1981, shortly after the election of Edward Seaga and his conservative government. The agency began promotional activities by focusing on image-building activities to some extent in an attempt to change the poor investment image that Jamaica had gained during the 1970s, when Michael Manley and his Socialist party were in power, but also because of the agency's lack of experience in investment promotion. Officials from the agency pointed out that many of the early decisions about which promotional techniques to use were based upon trial and error. Thus, although more general promotional techniques were used in these early years, the techniques were expected both to change Jamaica's unfavorable investment image and to generate investment.

By the mid-1980s, the JNIP had become convinced that a targeted approach was the most effective way of generating investment. The agency moved to a promotional effort that revolved around direct mail campaigns, firm-specific research, and visits to targeted companies. The JNIP continued to advertise in selected sectoral media, but it expected most investment leads to come from personal contacts with corporations.

Four agencies did not begin their promotional operations by focusing on image-building activities, then shifting to a focus on investment-generating activities. One of these, Indonesia's BKPM, did begin investment promotion operations by focusing on image-building activities, although, as in several previous cases, this stage was not thought of as such by officials at the BKPM. The agency's primary promotional technique was the general investment mission. In early 1988, the BKPM had not yet moved to a focus on investment-generating activities, although at that time there were indications that the consulting firms that had been engaged to promote investment were beginning to use investment-generating techniques primarily in their promotional efforts.

The other three agencies, Singapore's EDB, Malaysia's MIDA, and Scotland's LIS, all seemed to have started their investment promotion activities in an investment-generating mode. The case of LIS is exceptional in that it was in a position to benefit from the image-building activities of Britain's IBB. LIS executives considered that image building for all of Britain was an important function for the IBB.

The EDB and MIDA were two of the first organizations to promote investment actively. MIDA began active promotion during the early 1970s, some three years after its formation—actually the formation of its predecessor organization, FIDA, in 1967. The EDB began active investment promotion activities during the late 1960s. In both instances, several years passed between the formation of these organizations and the beginning of a focus on investment-generating activities. It is not clear whether the period that preceded a focus on investment-generating activities was spent in the attempt to build an image, or whether it consisted of passive rather than active promotional efforts. In the absence of evidence to the contrary, we have had to assume that these agencies did not begin investment promotion operations in an image-building stage.

Although in the case of MIDA there is no clear evidence of an initial focus on image building, the early years of the organization were certainly characterized by efforts to build an image in the investment community, in conjunction with attempts to generate investment directly.

In MIDA's early years, the principal investment-generating technique was specific investment missions to capital-exporting countries. Especially prominent were the missions to the electronics sector of the United States. Preceding these missions, specific companies in fast-growing sectors such as semiconductors had been identified, and during the mission discussions would be held between senior government officials and executives of these companies. The missions also included more general seminars, however, that may have served an image-building function. In these seminars, government ministers would give speeches and representatives from several government departments would discuss the available incentives that had recently been legislated and hold question and answer sessions.

In sum, the empirical evidence on the existence of separate emphases on image building and investment generation in the sequence we propose is quite strong. Seven of the ten agencies that were studied began investment promotion operations in an image-building mode. Of these seven agencies, six shifted, in time, to an investment-generating mode. At the time of the study the seventh was in a position to move to an emphasis on investment generation.

There is also evidence to support the logic that we propose as an explanation for this particular sequence of stages. Three of the agencies support the view that agencies shift from a focus on image building when they feel that appropriate images of their country have been built either in the minds of the larger investment community, or in those of targeted groups of investors. The other three agencies provide at least partial support for the alternative proposition that agencies move from an image-building focus to an investment-generating focus as they learn more about investment promotion. We nevertheless conclude that the weight of the evidence, from empirical observations and from the literature in industrial marketing, points to an explanation and a logic for separate emphases on image building and investment generation in a particular sequence. But learning from mistakes is also clearly a factor.

The Function of Targeting in an Investment Promotion Strategy

In all the agencies that shifted from a focus on image-building activities to a focus on investment-generating activities, this shift corresponded with the use of more closely targeted promotional techniques. As promotion agencies move from an emphasis on image building to an emphasis on investment generation, the audience of the investment promotion program becomes more sharply focused.

The idea of targeting is used here in a broad sense. Promotion agencies can target either a particular type of investor or a particular type of project for investment. In targeting a particular type of investor, agencies can target by industry. by sector, by geographical region, or by attributes of a class of investors—for example, size, growth rate, export intensity of production, labor intensity of production, level of technology, value added of production, or any attribute that will identify a group of prospective investors that can be matched with the competitive advantages a particular country has to offer.

Most agencies use targeted approaches throughout their focus on investment generation. Malaysia's MIDA, however, presents an example of an agency whose promotional techniques became less closely targeted during the agency's focus on investment generation. MIDA claims to have had significant success from its initial specific investment missions during the early 1970s, especially the promotional efforts to attract the U.S. semiconductor industry.[12] Although MIDA continued to use investment missions as a vehicle to promote foreign investment, in time these missions became more general. Ministers had fewer meetings with company managers, and the emphasis appears to have moved to generation of as large an audience as possible for the events of the missions. In other words, MIDA moved from specific missions, which we have characterized as an investment-generating technique, to general missions, which we have characterized as an image-building technique. There is no evidence that the latter missions have led directly to the generation of investment.

Level of Development and Image-Building Techniques

Although all agencies, when their focus is on image building, use less closely targeted techniques than those used when the focus is on direct generation of investment, developing countries tend to use more targeted techniques than do industrial countries. The reason, we suggest, is that the less developed the country, the fewer the industries or types of firm that are likely to be attracted. Accordingly, for the less developed country a program that attempts to build an image indiscriminately across industries is likely to be wasteful of resources. Thus, an efficient program, even during a focus on image-building activities, is likely to be targeted toward a small number of industries.

Empirical observations provide relatively strong support for the foregoing proposition. The image-building activities of the agencies from three of the industrial countries in the sample, Investment Canada, Britain's IBB, Ireland's IDA, have certainly been more general than the image-building activities of the agencies from developing countries, Jamaica's JNIP, Costa Rica's CINDE, Malaysia's MIDA, and Indonesia's BKPM. The primary media used by the IBB at the beginning of its awareness campaign were the *Wall Street Journal, Business Week, Fortune,* and *The Economist.* As the campaign went on, other media, such as *Inc.,* were used to reach medium-size and smaller companies. Investment Canada used primarily general financial media in its image-building campaign, and Ireland's IDA has consistently focused on general financial media, such as *Business Week, Forbes, The Economist, Financial Times,* and the *Wall Street Journal.*

Scotland's LIS provides an exception in that the agency has relied almost exclusively on more closely targeted sectoral media, especially electronics publications. The agency's rationale for using sectoral, rather than general, financial media is that the territory receives broader coverage through the IBBs advertising in general media.

Jamaica's JNIP and Malaysia's MIDA have done much more limited and less frequent advertising than the agencies from industrial countries, and where advertising has been done, it has been primarily in media aimed at particular industrial sectors. The JNIP has advertised in sector-specific media such as *Womens Wear Daily* (apparel), and *Grower & Packer* (agribusiness). The agency has also organized general seminars and general investment missions and has participated in investment exhibitions. MIDA has used general missions and seminars as an image-building activity, although the agency feels that such missions have small investment-generating possibilities. Costa Rica continues to participate in investment exhibitions because of their image-building possibilities.

Agencies from two developing countries provide exceptions to the general pattern we observed. We indicated earlier that the promotional campaign developed by Thailand's BOI was an exception. The other agency to use general media advertising on a large scale was the Singapore EDB. In 1986 the EDB, an agency that until then had done very little advertising, engaged in an ad hoc advertising program using general financial media. The campaign was conducted in the aftermath of an economic recession in Singapore and was aimed at reminding a broad group of investors about Singapore's attractions as a location for foreign direct investment. The Singapore government regarded continued promotion of a wide spectrum of foreign investment as integral to a strategy of leading the country out of recession. The agency's officials felt that, given the broad spectrum of firms that had been attracted to Singapore during the two preceding decades, general financial media provided the only logical forum for a campaign designed to restore Singapore's image of competitiveness in the wake of the recession.

The case of the Singapore EDB was, in a sense, an exception that supported the pattern we observed of developing countries using less closely targeted image-building techniques because, out of necessity, they were courting a narrower audience of prospective investors. Singapore had been more successful in attracting a broad range of international investors than virtually any other developing country, with the possible exception of some of the country's East Asian neighbors. Indeed, it is the only developing country we know of that has the stated intention of becoming an industrial country by the turn of the century.[13]

It could be argued that, given the high costs associated with the most general image-building techniques, the patterns we observed could be explained by a comparison of the resources of the two groups of countries. Our discussions with promotional officials engaged in image-building activities does not support this interpretation of the pattern or its implication that, given additional resources, developing countries would find it cost-effective to use more general image-building techniques than the techniques they now use.

Further, lessons from research on the way corporations are most successful in building images provides some evidence for the importance of developing countries engaging in targeted image-building programs.[14] Through recent research in marketing, the task corporations face in building an image in the eyes of key decisionmakers is seen as the corporate positioning problem. This image-building activity has two dimensions: visibility, or the breadth of the company's reputation, and credibility, or the quality of the company's reputation among those executives that know it.

In examining the interaction between visibility and credibility, Kosnik has shown that companies fall into four general categories, as depicted in table 5.

The framework suggests that companies with low credibility and low visibility should first build credibility in selected market segments, then engage in high-visibility activities; that is, companies should move from an "unknown" state to an "undiscovered" state, finally seeking to become "unparalleled." Kosnik notes that companies should avoid an "undesirable" state. In such a situation, a company has high visibility from a failure and no one in the marketplace willing to vouch for its credibility. Such a company would find it very difficult to recover and build a strong image.

We suggest that the parallels between companies building images as marketers of industrial products and countries building images as attractive investment sites are close. Many developing countries do not have strong reputations as attractive sites for investment. It seems imperative that these countries, like companies in similar situations, build credibility among a targeted group of investors before broadening their image-building efforts.

Table 5. A Framework for Comparing Visibility and Credibility

| | Visibility | |
Credibility	Low	High
High	Undiscovered	Unparalleled
Low	Unknown	Undesirable

Source: Thomas J. Kosnik, "Corporate Positioning: How to Assess—and Build—a Company's Reputation," working paper (Boston: Harvard Business School, 1988).

In sum, the model discussed in this chapter provides a framework for understanding the mix of targeted and general techniques in investment promotion that we observed in many cases. Investment promotion agencies tend to focus separately on image building or on investment generation.

All agencies tend to use relatively general promotional techniques during their focus on image building. Several agencies from developing countries, however, tend to use image-building techniques that are less general than do agencies from industrial countries. These agencies are usually courting a narrower range of prospective investors and, accordingly, like corporations that engage in successful image-building activities, they seek to build credibility among a narrow group of investors before engaging in more visible image-building activities.

Research in industrial marketing suggests that impersonal promotional techniques are most effective during the early stages of the industrial buying decision process and that personal techniques are more effective during the later stages of the industrial buying decision process. The investment decision process is very similar to the industrial buying process, so it is not surprising that a similar relationship holds in investment promotion.

Agencies move from a focus on image building to a focus on investment generation in an attempt to adapt to the decision processes of their customers. Agencies focus on image building when most of the investors they hope to attract can be expected to be in the early stages of the investment decision process. They move to a focus on investment generation when a majority of prospective investors are in the later stages of the investment decision process. In shifting the focus from image building to investment generation, agencies tend to adopt more closely targeted promotional techniques that rely on personal contact with companies.

We found that promotional organizations were not equally adept at making the transition from the use of general and impersonal techniques to the use of more closely targeted and personal approaches. Certain organizational structures facilitated this transition to a greater extent than others. These differences in structure are the subject of the following chapter.

Notes

1. See Gerard B. Watzke, "An Irish Sweepstakes for American Corporations," *Journal of General Management,* Summer 1982, 35, for an analysis suggesting that part of the success of the Industrial Development Authority (IDA) of Ireland is the result of its targeted promotion efforts and International Policy Analysis, SRI International-Washington, *An Assessment of Investment Promotion Activities* (Washington: SRI International, 1984) for a similar conclusion about the importance of targeted promotion based on an examination of the investment promotion programs of Ireland, Jamaica, Egypt, and Costa Rica.

2. See International Policy Analysis, *Assessment of Investment,* p. 48.

3. This anomaly will be discussed in greater detail in chapter 4, in the context of an evaluation of the effectiveness of image-building activities.

4. This is the most common typology in industrial marketing, and is credited to the work of Robinson and his colleagues, who developed a typology of buying situations or "buyclasses," namely, the "new task" (first purchase), the "straight rebuy" (routine reorder from seller of first purchase), and the "modified rebuy" (modified buying specifications with competition for reorder from several sellers). See Patrick J. Robinson, Charles W. Faris, and Yoram Wind, *Industrial Buying and Creative Marketing* (Boston: Allyn and Bacon, 1967); and Yoram Wind and Patrick J. Robinson, "Simulating the Industrial Buying Process," in *Marketing and the New Science of Planning,* ed. Robert L King (Chicago: American Marketing Association, Fall Conference Proceedings, 1968) for a complete discussion of this typology.

5. This area of research has developed within behavioral explanations of the organizational buying process. It began with the innovation-adoption paradigm that sought to explain how organizations adopted new products and services. For this original model, see Everett M. Rodgers, *Diffusion*

of Innovations (New York: The Free Press, 1962), p.306; and Everett M. Rodgers and F. Floyd Shoemaker, *Communication of Innovation: A Cross-Cultural Approach* (New York: The Free Press, 1971). The paradigm was extended to explain the way industrial and institutional buyers purchase new products and to identify the sources of information most appropriate at each stage of the purchase decision. For the application of the model to industrial marketing, see Urban B. Ozanne and Gilbert A. Churchill, Jr., "Adoption Research: Information Sources in the Industrial Purchase Decision," in *Marketing and the New Science of Planning*, ed. King, p. 353; Urban B. Ozanne and Gilbert A. Churchill, Jr., "Five Dimensions of the Industrial Adoption Process," *Journal of Marketing Research* 8 (1971): 322–28; F. E. Webster, Jr., Interpersonal Communication and Salesman Effectiveness," *Journal of Marketing* 3 (1968): 7–13; and John A. Martilla, "Word of Mouth Communication in the Industrial Adoption Proces," *Journal of Marketing Research* 8 (May 1971): 173–78. For the application of the model to institutional marketing, see Leon G. Shiffman, Leon Winer, and Vincent Gaccione, "The Role of Sources of Information in the Institutional Buying Decision-Making Process," in *Foundations of Marketing Channels,* Arch G. Woodside et al. (Austin, Texas: Lone Star Publishers, 1978), pp.248–263. The model has also had widespread appeal in more popular and current industrial marketing literature. For current references to this model, see Rowland T. Moriarty, *Industria Buying Behavior: Concepts, Issues, and Applications* (Lexington: Lexington Books 1983) p. 26; and Philip Kotler, *Marketing Management: Analysis, Planning and Control* (Englewood Cliffs, New Jersey: Prentice Hall, 1984), p. 165.

6. See Rodgers, *Diffusion of Innovations,* p. 307; and Ozanne and Churchill, "Adoption Research," p. 353.

7. See Robinson et al., *Industrial Buying.*

8. See Robert W. Haas, *Industrial Marketing Management* (Boston: Kent Publishing Company, 1986).

9. See Investment Canada, *Annual Report,* June30, 1985–March 31, 1986 (Ottawa: Ministry of Supply and Services, 1986). p.21.

10. Quoted from Industrial Development Authority of Ireland, *Annual Report* (Dublin 1970–71).

11. See Invest in Britain Bureau, *Annual Report,* (London Department of Trade and Industry 1985), p.12.

12. In 1987 Malaysia was the world's largest exporter and third largest producer of semiconductors. MIDA officials take credit for significantly influencing the first semiconductor forms, such as National Semiconductor, that set up operations in Malaysia through the use of specific investment missions to the West Coast of the United States during the early 1970s. See Malaysian Industrial Development Authority, *20th Anniversary,* October 1987, pp.29, 33.

13. For a complete treatment of the causes of the Singapore recession and the importance of foreign direct investment in restoring growth and achieving the country's objective of becoming an industrial country before the turn of the century, see the report of the Economic Committee, *The Singapore Economy: New Directions* (Singapore: Ministry of Trade and Industry, February 1986), pp. 1–20.

14. In this section we have drawn heavily on the work of Kosnik, whose research has been focused on industrial marketing to high-technology firms. See Thomas J. Kosnik, "Corporate Positioning: How to Assess—and Build—a Company's Reputation," Working Paper (Boston: Harvard Business School, 1988).

3

The Appropriate Organization for Promotion: Public, Private, or Other?

The central issue faced by governments in *organizing* to promote foreign direct investment appears to be the appropriate mix of public and private sector involvement in the investment promotion function. Investment promotion involves some tasks usually handled by private organizations—the marketing task, for example—and others more typical of traditional government organizations, such as the function of servicing investors. Accordingly, the investment promotion function, like several other nontraditional government activities studied in other situations, can benefit from the skills and resources of both the private and the public sectors. It is these characteristics of the investment promotion activity that create a problem of choice for the government.

This central issue is quite different from that in the more extensive literature on the way governments organize to *negotiate* with foreign investors. That literature has been dominated by the issue of whether the government's negotiating function should be handled by a centralized organization, by an organization that coordinates various agencies, or by several government agencies or ministries.[1]

In examining the ways governments organize to *promote* foreign direct investment, however, we discovered that centralization versus decentralization seemed not to be a contentious issue. Countries that promote foreign direct investment use primarily centralized or coordinated organizational structures. Table 6 indicates that in all sixteen of the countries that were actively involved in promoting foreign investment, and for which we had data, responsibility for the promotion of investment resided in a single organization.

Decisions on promotion and decisions on screening and negotiation have different degrees of effect on the interests of line ministries. It is this fact that leads to the differences in the importance of centralization. Since the outcome of negotiations and screening

Table 6. Organizations with Responsibility for Investment Promotion

Locality	Organization with primary responsibility for investment promotion
Jamaica	Jamaica National Investment Promotion (JNIP)
Ireland	Industrial Development Authority (IDA)
Singapore	Economic Development Board (EDB)
Malaysia	Malaysia Industrial Development Authority (MIDA)
Thailand	Thailand Board of Investment (BOI)
Costa Rica	Costa Rican Investment Promotion Program (CINDE)
Britain	Invest in Britain Bureau (IBB)
Barbados	Barbados Industrial Development Corporation
St. Lucia	St. Lucia Industrial Development Corporation
Hong Kong	Hong Kong Government Industry Department
Israel	Israel Investment Authority
France	French Industrial Development Agency
Austria	Industrial Cooperation and Development Austria
Canada	Investment Canada
Indonesia	Investment Coordinating Board (BKPM)
Scotland	Locate in Scotland

can lead to direct effects on their activities, ministries are eager to have a say in negotiations and in the investment-screening process. They are less concerned if they are excluded from efforts to attract investors, since the mere interest of a potential investor offers little threat. Accordingly, it is politically easier to transfer all authority to attract investors to one organization than to transfer all authority to one organization for negotiation and screening.[2]

Types of Organization for Investment Promotion

While investment promotion is consistently centralized, there are important organizational choices to be made. In some instances, the responsible organization is purely a government entity, subject to civil service rules and practices. In others, the organization is "quasi government," established outside the normal civil service rules and practices. In fact, in one instance the organization was actually private (see table 7).

In their attempts to organize for investment promotion, governments face a problem: the task of promotion has some of the attributes of tasks normally performed by public organizations and

Table 7. Organizing for Investment Promotion

Locality	Promotion agency	Type of organization
Britain	Invest in Britain Bureau	Government
Canada	Investment Canada	Government
Costa Rica	Costa Rican Investment Promotion Program	Private
Indonesia	Investment Coordinating Board	Government
Ireland	Industrial Development Authority	Quasi-government
Jamaica	Jamaica National Investment Promotion	Quasi-government
Malaysia	Malaysian Industrial Development Authority	Quasi-government
Scotland	Locate in Scotland	Quasi-government
Singapore	Economic Development Board	Quasi-government
Thailand	Board of Investment	Government

some of the attributes of tasks normally performed by private organizations. For this reason, we encountered three different approaches, each with different degrees of private and public sector involvement.

There are various reasons that promotion activities are generally performed by governments. Most important, the results of investment promotion activities are not readily captured in a form that would allow a private firm to earn a profit by conducting them. Investment promotion activities, to the extent that they are successful in helping to attract foreign direct investment, provide social benefits that outweigh their potential to generate private profits. Accordingly, like many other government activities, if these activities are not financed by the public sector it is likely that they will be underprovided.[3] Of course, the government could in theory pay to a private agency an amount that would reflect the social value of each firm that it attracts. The problems of measuring social benefits and of determining who was responsible for investment make such a solution impractical. Thus, public finance usually means a public organization. Although the investment promotion function is principally a marketing task, to be successful it requires close interaction with the government apparatus that screens investment and provides incentives for investors. In addition; investment promotion agencies conduct a service activity that involves assisting investors to gain the approvals and permits they require to implement their investments. All these functions require close interaction with government; this is probably easier if the agency is, in fact, a part of the government.

The principal task of an investment promotion function, however, is marketing a country as an investment site. This task is more similar to activities generally undertaken by private entities than to normal government business. The skills required are usually found in the private sector and can usually be had only for salaries typical of that sector, hence the difficulty of choice.

Some governments have chosen the purely government organization, and have tried to solve the problems inherent in that approach. As noted earlier, one country went to the other extreme and allowed a private organization to undertake the task. Many countries took a middle road, a "quasi-government" organization.

Government Organization for Investment Promotion

In government promotion agencies, the responsibility for investment promotion resided wholly within the normal government structure and civil service system. These organizations were typically

- departments within the ministry of industry, such as Britain's IBB;
- agencies such as Investment Canada that reported to the ministry of industry; or
- agencies organized under the prime minister's or president's office, such as Thailand's BOI and Indonesia's BKPM.

In spite of their slightly varying forms, the government agencies tended to exhibit a pattern. In three out of the four examples—Investment Canada, Thailand's BOI, and Indonesia's BKPM—the structures were initially created to screen foreign investment, and investment promotion was subsequently added to or, in the case of Investment Canada, replaced the original screening function of the organization.

Both the BOI and the BKPM were created to screen investment and negotiate with investors. The BOI, established in 1954, began promoting investment only during the early 1980s. In 1987 only one of the organization's eight divisions and 20 percent of the organization's staff were directly involved in investment promotion activities. Like the BOI, the BKPM was also established with the mandate to negotiate with foreign investors and screen foreign investment. Although the agency had sporadically undertaken minor promotion activities earlier, much like the BOI, the BKPM did not begin active investment promotion efforts until the early 1980s.

In 1987 only 8 percent of the agency's staff were directly involved in investment promotion activities.

In contrast to the BOI and the BKPM, Investment Canada was created with the explicit purpose of promoting investment. This agency, however, inherited its organizational structure from its predecessor, the Federal Investment Review Agency (FIRA), which was established to screen investment. Its structure was not changed with the transition to Investment Canada. Indeed, in many ways Investment Canada was only a continuation of FIRA with some changes in personnel and a major change in function. Investment Canada remained a part of the Canadian civil service, reporting directly to the "Minister responsible for Investment Canada."

Only Britain's IBB did not fit the pattern. The organization was originally created in 1977 explicitly to promote investment in selected regions of Britain. The IBB's function was expanded by the Thatcher government in 1980 to the promotion of investment in all regions of Britain. In spite of its history, it was a purely government organization, operating within the civil service structure.

The organizations that were set up with the primary function of screening foreign investment and negotiating with foreign investors were firmly enmeshed within the normal government structure, since screening foreign investment and negotiating with foreign investors are traditional government activities. When promotion is simply an added function, the organizational structure tends not to change.

Quasi-Government Organization for Investment Promotion

Although some countries organize investment promotion as they organize most other government functions, this seems to occur primarily when the structure is inherited from an organization created with the mandate of conducting the traditional government activities of screening and regulating. Where the assignment of promotion is elsewhere, the organizational structure is different. This is because investment promotion is significantly different from traditional government processes such as directing, controlling, and regulating, creating and administering laws, exercising authority, operating as a custodian, and so forth. Investment promotion is, in fact, more like activities typical of the private sector, particularly marketing. It requires a continuous liaison with the private sector; the flexibility to respond speedily to investors' needs, adjust to changing market conditions, and acquire scarce management skills; and the autonomy to generate and implement investment promotion strategies that are consistent throughout a long period.

Conventional government organizations are typically not very good at these tasks. They usually lack managers familiar with the private sector and with professional marketing practices, despite their prowess at traditional government functions. Further, government organizations are generally not flexible, nor are they sufficiently autonomous to chart policies without political interference from successive governments. Accordingly, in response to the perception of many governments that investment promotion is best conducted by a flexible, adaptive, and autonomous organization, the investment promotion programs of a number of countries were conducted through quasi-government agencies. It seemed that the countries adopting this organizational approach expected these agencies to find it easier than government organizations to take on characteristics, such as flexibility in hiring and firing, autonomy, and a concern with cost containment, that are normally associated with private organizations.

Quasi-government agencies typically have their own boards of directors, report to the ministry of industry without being part of that ministry, and recruit staff outside the regular civil service. The creation of such quasi-government organizations is consistent with the recommendations of some academics and consultants that countries adopt structures, for both investment and export promotion, that are flexible and autonomous.[4]

Five of the agencies that we studied were quasi-government organizations. All these agencies were either established for the primary purpose of promoting their countries as investment sites or changed their organizational structures when the principal function of the organization became investment promotion.

One of the agencies, Ireland's IDA, changed to a quasi-government structure to facilitate investment promotion activities. IDA was established in about 1949, within the Ministry of Industry and Commerce. The agency's function, however, was not clearly defined for its first twenty years of existence. During the 1960s the senior people of IDA began to have a more influential voice in government policymaking. They helped to steer the country away from a protectionist development strategy and toward one of freer trade. After this change in development policy, IDA began to take on a more proactive promotional function, and it influenced a few foreign companies to invest in Ireland. Once IDA began to engage in active investment promotion efforts, individuals within the IDA organization found that they were having difficulty communicating and developing relations with the private sector while operating directly out of the ministry.

During the mid- to late 1960s, the consulting firm Arthur D. Little, Inc. (ADL), was asked to examine the existing IDA organizational structure and to recommend a structure that would be the best one to achieve IDA's institutional objectives. ADL's report, submitted in 1968, suggested that there be a complete break between IDA and the Ministry of Industry and Commerce. ADL's conclusions are thought to have reflected the views of a majority of IDA officials at that time. By 1969, a new Industrial Development Act was legislated, and in 1970 IDA came into being in its present form. The agency was changed to a quasi-government agency, with its own Board of Directors, operating outside the civil service but financed by the Ministry of Industry and Commerce, to which it ultimately reported. It was felt that the new structure would allow flexibility and the ability to make rapid decisions much more typical of a private company than of a government bureaucracy.

Three of the quasi-government agencies in the sample—in Singapore, Scotland, and Jamaica—began investment promotion activities as quasi-government agencies and continued them in that form. Singapore's EDB was an autonomous public organization. Classified as a statutory body, the agency had more flexibility in setting salaries than government ministries that were a part of the civil service. The EDB had its own board, most of the members of which were appointed from Singapore's private sector. Locate in Scotland (LIS) was the international arm of the Scottish Development Administration (SDA). LIS was a joint venture between the Industry Department of Scotland and the SDA and combined the powers of both of these organizations. The SOA, described as a nondepartment public body, was a quasi-govermnent organization, operating outside the civil service. The organization paid salaries that were 20 to 40 percent higher than civil service salaries. In 1987 36 percent of the SDA's income came from commercial activities. Jamaica's JNIP was set up in 1981 as a quasi-government organization. The agency existed outside the regular civil service, paid salaries much higher than civil service salaries, and also had its own Board of Directors, the members of which came primarily from the private sector.

The fifth quasi-government agency, Malaysia's MIDA, was the one agency that, although formally maintaining its original quasi-government structure, seemed to have lost some of its autonomy in the course of its work. Following the recommendations of a World Bank study, the agency was established in 1967 as an autonomous, quasi-government organization. In its early years, MIDA, then called Federal Industrial Development Authority (FIDA), was a powerful, autonomous agency. Part of its power came from a mandate from the government to generate economic growth through foreign investment. During the late 1960s, the need for economic growth was critical because of the government's attempts to restructure the economy so as to distribute wealth to the Malay majority in the wake of the race riots in Malaysia in 1969. The government's goal was to increase the Malay share of the national economic wealth from the 2 percent that it was during the late 1960s to 30 percent by 1990. It was decided that the transfer of wealth should take place out of increased national wealth rather than by taking wealth away from the Chinese minority. The government's objectives in the distribution and creation of wealth were summarized in its New Economic Policy (NEP). The NEP has had a profound effect on government and economic policy in Malaysia since 1970.

It was in the supportive political environment of the early 1970s, when the government's emphasis was on the creation of wealth, that a powerful, autonomous, entrepreneurial FIDA organization engineered the strategic studies and coordinated the specific investment missions that were focused on attracting American semiconductor manufacturers to Malaysia. Some would argue, however, that after this period, MIDI's autonomy steadily decreased, as the agency was forced to operate within an increasingly stifling political environment. These maintain that throughout the decade of the 1970s, the country's raw materials fetched strong world market prices, making the attraction of investment less important. Further, without the need for promotion, other electronic firms followed the first few firms that had invested in Malaysia. The government's adherence to the NEP continued unabated, but in a prospering economy the tools to meet these objectives shifted from policies geared to the creation of wealth to policies geared to the distribution of wealth. Thus, MIDI's autonomy lessened as the agency became increasingly constrained by government restructuring regulations.[5] It was felt that this reduced autonomy may have reduced the effectiveness with which MIDA was able to promote investment and attract qualified personnel.

During MIDA'S formative years, for instance, competitive salaries helped it to attract some of the country's best university graduates. Salaries then were purportedly 45 percent higher than normal civil service salaries and even higher than salaries in the private sector. In time, however, there was an equalizing of salaries between MIDA and the civil service, so by 1987 MIDA salaries were equivalent to civil service salaries, and both were well below private sector salaries. As a consequence, MIDA found it more difficult to compete with the private sector for the country's best graduates in the 1980s than it had twenty years before.

All five quasi-government organizations seemed able to merge skills typical of both the public and private sectors as long as they maintained their autonomy. The flexibility they enjoyed allowed them to acquire with relative ease the marketing skills necessary for investment promotion, and their relations with the formal government hierarchy allowed them to serve investors and perform other functions that required close relations with the traditional government structure. As organizations not judged by profit performance, they were able to keep social goals in their targets.

Private Organization for Investment Promotion

One of the agencies in the sample was created as a more radical response to the fact that investment promotion is a nontraditional government function that may require a nontraditional structure.

In 1987 the Costa Rican investment promotion agency, CINDE, was a private organization, with no direct connections or reporting relations to any ministry or other government organization. Investment promotion in Costa Rica had not, however, always resided wholly within the private sector. In 1982, as a part of its Private Sector Development Initiative within Costa Rica, the United States Agency for International Development (USAID) attempted to begin an investment promotion function in Costa Rica. Two organizations, both of which USAID had helped to create, were given the mandate to promote foreign investment: a private organization, CINDE, and an organization that before 1986 was a quasi-government organization, MINEX. Neither organization was successful in attracting investment during the period 1982–84.

By 1984 the lack of success of either MINEX or CINDE in attracting investment led to attempts to identify investment promotion experts who could provide guidance for Costa Rica's investment promotion program. As a result, in that year a consultant from Ireland's IDA arrived in Costa Rica and began to make suggestions about the way investment promotion should be conducted. He recommended an approach that relied primarily upon aggressive personal selling to certain targeted firms. The IDA consultant initially attempted to implement his targeted approach to investment promotion through MINEX. This organization was hesitant, however, and because of this hesitancy the investment promotion program, in its entirety, was transferred to CINDE. The agency's experiences in conducting investment promotion have suggested some of the potential advantages and disadvantages of locating the investment promotion function wholly outside the public sector.

CINDE was able to attract highly qualified, motivated employees and keep them working at high levels of productivity partly because of the organization's ability to pay attractive salaries and offer generous financial bonuses. CINDE employees earned salaries that were at least three or four times those of their government counterparts. For above average performance, promotion officials stationed overseas could receive financial bonuses equal to as much as 13 percent of their base salaries. The CINDE organization also had more latitude in hiring and firing employees than the typical government organization. In instances, albeit rare ones, CINDE employees were fired or relocated if their performance fell below expectations. The fact that employees could be fired for poor performance, coupled with the positive reinforcement of valuable financial incentives, created high levels of productivity, especially on the part of overseas promotion staff.

On the other hand, as a private organization, CINDE found it more difficult to develop working relations with Costa Rican government organizations. Government officials were not involved at senior levels of CINDE, as evidenced by the fact that in 1987 there was no government representative on CINDE's Board of Directors. The agency was, it is suggested by some investors, less successful in providing services for investors than in other aspects of promoting investment. This was possibly because it did not have the same access to government departments involved in approving permits, and the like, that a government or quasi-government promotion organization would have and also because of an evaluation structure that rewarded only effort devoted to attracting firms.

In 1987 CINDE took a step toward strengthening its weak relations with the Costa Rican government. During that year the agency signed a two-year collaboration agreement with the Ministry of Foreign Affairs, which helped CINDE gain official status with foreign governments for its investment promoters working abroad.

Another facet of this agreement into which CINDE reluctantly entered was the use of diplomatic personnel in some sections of the world as part-time investment promoters. According to this agreement, CINDE was to recruit several employees from within the Costa Rican foreign service and train them as investment promoters. These persons would staff the investment promotion function of six embassies. These new overseas offices would complement the agency's existing network of "stand-alone" investment promotion offices. The employees would be given specific budgets for investment promotion activities and communications equipment, such as personal computers and facsimile machines, which would allow them to be integrated into the CINDE information network. To motivate performance, these promoters were to be given significant incentives related to the number of foreign investors they were able to attract to Costa Rica. The incentives would be sufficiently high that an above-average performer would be able to double his foreign service salary. These promoters would report to CINDE's regional promoter, who would, in turn, report the results achieved by each office in his region, including any embassy offices, in the quarterly reports that were sent to CINDE's headquarters in San Jose. In 1988 preliminary evaluations of this experiment indicated that it had not been particularly successful.

Despite the success that has been attributed to CINDE by various groups within the Costa Rican government and private sector, there were still many in government who thought that the CINDE structure was not the ideal arrangement for investment promotion and that the Costa Rican government should be more involved in promoting Costa Rica abroad.

The case of Costa Rica was unusual since CINDE was financed wholly by USAID, a situation made possible because of the United States's geopolitical objectives in Central America, in general, and in Costa Rica in particular. As we have pointed out, in theory, any government could finance investment promotion operations while allowing the promotional function to be managed by a private organization. Indeed, the decade of the 1980s has seen a tremendous increase in the privatization of a variety of activities that were previously managed by governments.[6] Nevertheless, public funding with private control is likely, in practice, to be unacceptable in many countries. The kind of pressure CINDE faced from the government is likely to be overwhelming if financing is not provided from sources other than the local government.

The experience of CINDE does point out that a private organization for investment promotion is likely to entail the costs of a reduced ability to conduct the public aspects of the investment promotion function, coupled with the proportionately greater benefits of an enhanced ability to conduct the private aspects of investment promotion. Government organizations offer the opposite strengths and weaknesses. The quasi-government agencies that we studied, however, seemed to provide a reasonable compromise for the investment promotion function. They were better able than private organizations to perform the tasks of promotion that seem suited to public sector organizations, yet they were also able to acquire the skills and expertise necessary to conduct the aspects of investment promotion that are more like private sector activities, including the important function of overseas marketing.

Organizing for Overseas Marketing

Whether the country decides on a government organization, a quasi-government organization, or a private organization to carry out investment promotion, the organization must decide whether to have an overseas presence and, if so, what form that presence will take.

The choice of presence or no presence is largely a result of the focus of a country's promotional program. Image-building and investment-service activities do not require a permanent overseas presence. Effective investment-generating activities, however, seem to demand a permanent overseas presence. Thus agencies that are focusing on investment generation must have some form of permanent representation abroad.

As agencies such as Costa Rica's CINDE, Investment Canada, Britain's IBB, Ireland's IDA, and Jamaica's JNIP moved from a focus on image building to a focus on investment generation, a greater emphasis was placed on organizing an effective, permanent overseas marketing presence.

If a presence is to be established, the form of that overseas presence typically follows from the type of organization at home that is responsible for investment promotion, whether government or quasi-government.

Overseas Marketing in Government Organizations

Investment promotion organizations established within the ambit of the normal government and civil service system have tended to regard the entire promotion function as a traditional government function. These agencies have, accordingly, seen fit to conduct overseas marketing through the country's network of consulates or embassies.

In 1987 all four government agencies in the sample—Investment Canada, Britain's IBB, Thailand's BOI, and Indonesia's BKPM—conducted overseas marketing through consulates or embassies. For the BKPM, this had not always been the case. Between 1983 and 1986, the BKPM had three investment promotion offices overseas, in Paris, Frankfurt, and New York. The offices were physically located within offices of Hill and Knowlton, the U.S. public relations firm that represented the Indonesian government. They were passive operations, primarily responding to requests from investors for information. In 1986, in response to a growing sentiment that the offices were generating no investment, they were closed and the funds that had been used to finance their operations were used to add an investment promotion component to the functions of twelve economic consuls in Indonesian consulates and embassies overseas.

The other three government organizations, the IBB, Investment Canada, and the BOI, had always conducted investment promotion activities through the network of consulates and embassies of their respective countries.

Officials from government organizations suggested certain advantages they felt their organizations gained by conducting overseas marketing activities through consulates and embassies. One apparent advantage, as the Indonesian example illustrates, is that promotional resources can be spread over a broader geographical area. In the Indonesian case, the funds that had been used to support three investment promotion offices were later used to support investment promotion activities in twelve locations. An official from one government agency suggested another advantage: since a country's embassies and consulates are well known, investors might approach an embassy when they might never be aware of the existence or the location of a promotion office standing alone.

There are several disadvantages to this particular form of organization for overseas marketing, however. Although promotional resources might be spread over a broader geographical area, this is often achieved by using part-time rather than full-time investment promoters. Government organizations do not spend more on investment promotion; they simply spread their resources more thinly. The relative effectiveness of these alternative ways of spreading promotional resources is ultimately an empirical question. Our observations suggest that in situations in which investment promotion is a part-time activity of consular officials, there is a substantial risk that promotional activities will receive little attention. Investment promotion is a difficult marketing endeavor to implement, and results are difficult to measure. In situations in which it is a subsidiary function of the individual—or of an organization—

there is a tendency to ignore it and concentrate on the primary function or on an easier function.[7]

The risk that diplomatic staff will not emphasize promotional activities is exacerbated because of two typical, although by no means necessary, characteristics of the government organization that promotes foreign investment through diplomatic channels. The first is that diplomatic staff are normally trained as diplomats, have had little experience in industrial development, business, or marketing, and do not tend to be predisposed toward aggressive marketing. The second is that government organizations often do not develop comprehensive reporting and control systems between the organization at home and the diplomatic offices. Government promotion organizations can generally offer no incentives to motivate and reward the effort of consular officials, nor do they have power to control performance. In many situations no information system exists to make it possible even to evaluate performance.

That these are not necessary characteristics of government organizations is illustrated by the example of the Canadian promotional program that spent considerable time and effort in developing a management control system to monitor the performance of diplomatic staff.

Development of a Management Control System. In 1987 the Canadian investment promotion program was in the middle of an attempt to institute a comprehensive information and evaluation system to improve the productivity of diplomatic staff engaged in investment promotion activities. Although Investment Canada was the agency principally responsible for promoting investment in Canada, this agency worked very closely with the Department of External Affairs (DEA), which was responsible in part for investment promotion activities conducted at the "posts" (consulates or embassies), and the Department of Regional and Industrial Expansion (DRIE), which was responsible in part for providing sectoral expertise in the targeting and other industry- or sector-specific functions of investment promotion. The DEA developed a comprehensive tracking system designed to monitor and evaluate the performance of consular officials involved in all DEA functions, such as trade promotion, tourism, and investment promotion. DEA officials felt that the process of government had to become more disciplined and that this would happen only if government officials were held accountable for their efforts and the associated results or lack of results. This was the rationale for the development of the tracking system.

The Canadian system included a planning component, which functioned in advance of each fiscal year. At the beginning of each year a package of materials would be sent to each post. The posts all contained at least three sections: export promotion, investment promotion, and tourism. Each of these sections was expected to complete a report. The priorities for the coming year and the results expected were to be included in the report. Investment promotion sections were to indicate how they planned to identify and develop potential investment opportunities and the quantity of investment they planned to achieve for the year. They were required to provide analyses of the external environment, indicating, for instance, why companies from this particular territory would seek to go abroad, and what group of companies might be most interested in investing in Canada. On the basis of the forms submitted from posts all over the world, the DEA would put together a sectoral and geographical investment promotion program for the forthcoming year.

The DEA's tracking system took fourteen months to develop and came on line in November 1986. In conjunction with Investment Canada, the DEA in 1987 was working on a more elaborate tracking system for investment promotion that would enable all promotional contacts to be tied to eventual investment decisions. In the interim, investment activity was recorded on Business Activity Forms, which also indicated what promotional technique had led to initial contacts with the prospective investor.

As this description demonstrates, the Canadian promotional program made intense efforts to counteract what the agency saw as problems that often afflict government organizations—namely, lack of motivation and accountability on the part of employees. Most government promotion organizations do not make such efforts, and in their absence it becomes very difficult for these organizations to monitor, evaluate, and motivate the performance of diplomatic promotion staff.

Overseas Marketing in Quasi-Government Organizations

In contrast to government agencies, quasi-government agencies have tended to establish elaborate networks of overseas promotional offices that stand alone, independent of their countries' networks of consulates or embassies. The principal advantage of this organizational form is that overseas marketers are typically full-time investment promoters. The quasi-government agency can recruit employees specifically to perform the function of investment promotion. This, coupled with the flexibility these organizations tend to enjoy, allows the agencies to employ persons who possess the skills and training investment promotion requires.

In the agencies of this sort that we observed, overseas marketers reported only to the home office. This appears to explain why quasi-government agencies tended to devote more effort to the development of information and control systems than did government agencies. The one exception was the case of Canada where the agencies involved in investment promotion devoted considerable effort to the development of a comprehensive information and control system.

Since quasi-government agencies do not rely on existing networks of diplomatic offices, they are at an apparent disadvantage to government agencies in the scope of overseas promotional representation. Quasi-government agencies have, however, demonstrated their commitment to investment promotion by building an impressive network of stand-alone promotional offices. Table 8 provides some indication of the scope of the overseas networks of these agencies as of 1987.

Table 8. Overseas Promotion Network of Quasi-Government Agencies

Promotion agency	Number of overseas offices	Number of countries	Number of continents
Costa Rican Investment Promotion Program (CINDE)[a]	7	4	3
Industrial Development Authority (IDA)	22	11	4
Jamaica National Investment Promotion (JNIP)	9	6	3
Malaysian Industrial Development Authority (MIDA)	12	10	4
Locate in Scotland (LIS)	7	4	3
Economic Development Board (EDB)	20	10	4

a. In this table, and whenever there was little, if any, distinction between the one case of private organization, and the several cases of quasi-government organization, the CINDE agency has been classified as a quasi-government agency, since it was similar in many respects to these organizations.

Incorporating Private Sector Skills into Investment Promotion

Conventional government organizations do not easily attract the skills or adopt the attitudes appropriate to some of the tasks of investment promotion. For these organizations, a shift to the investment-generating stage of an investment promotion program usually brings into sharp relief the need for private sector marketing skills, and an external search for such skills is often initiated.

In search of skills normally located in the private sector, government agencies have done several things. Some have contracted with private organizations to perform either an entire set of investment promotion activities or one minor segment of an investment promotion operation. Other agencies have made special efforts to attract managers from the private sector through secondment programs.

Subcontracting Investment Promotion Activities to the Private Sector

Government and quasi-government agencies routinely acquire specialized private sector skills by subcontracting certain investment promotion activities. Both types of agency, for example, tend to contract out the image-building activities of advertising and public relations. This is because of the highly specialized nature of the skills required to conduct these activities.[8]

In contrast to image-building activities, which both government and quasi-government agencies contract out to private firms, there tends to be a sharp difference between government and quasi-government agencies in the extent to which investment-generating activities are contracted out to private organizations. Whereas quasi-government agencies are usually able to recruit into the organization people with the marketing skills required to conduct investment-generating activities, government agencies tend to contract out these activities to obtain marketing skills that are not available in-house. Since government agencies are most interested in gaining access to a comprehensive overseas marketing network that will aid in the identification of prospective investors, these agencies often contract with foreign firms.

The contracting out of government activities to private firms is not unique to investment promotion. Contracting for private sector expertise, one method of transferring activities previously managed by the government to the private sector (or privatization), is a common approach used by governments, from city to federal, to conduct a variety of nontraditional government functions.[9]

Contracting is often advocated as the appropriate privatization choice in situations in which it is imperative that the government continue to finance the operation but it is also felt that some aspects of the operation might benefit from management by the private sector. Advocates of the contracting out of government activities to the private sector point out that this procedure reduces costs because, assuming that contractors are chosen through competitive bidding, market forces will ensure that the contractors provide services more efficiently than monopolistic public agencies. Contracting out is particularly appropriate, it is argued, when public agencies need to acquire specialized skills offered by the private sector but possibly unavailable within the government. These skills are not necessarily better than public sector management skills; they are simply different.[10]

In many respects investment promotion fits the description of a government activity that could benefit from being contracted out to the private sector. It requires government financing because of the discrepancy between private profit and social benefit; in that sense it is a public function, yet for some tasks it also requires marketing expertise that is likely to be in short supply in the public sector, and it can perhaps be made more cost-effective through market competition that can be inserted through the contracting-out process.

There are, however, potential problems in subcontracting government activities. Contracting has been associated with excessive costs in instances in which contractors were not subject to competitive pressures. Further, it is often difficult for a public manager to ensure that a contractor is meeting the terms of the contract, because for many government activities that are contracted out it is easier to measure costs than benefits. This is particularly true in situations in which the goals of the organization include certain social objectives. Given that this issue of performance evaluation has dominated the literature on state-owned enterprises (SOEs), it is not surprising that it is also often difficult to evaluate the performance of contractors engaged in certain government activities).[11]

In investment promotion, however, some of the problems often associated with evaluation of the performance of public operations need not apply. While it is certainly true that the results of particular promotional activities are difficult to measure, the primary objectives of the investment-generating phase of an investment promotion program are usually quite clear and quantifiable. Accordingly, it is possible to set objectives for an investment-generating activity, whether they be for site visits, applications, or jobs.

Further, the performance of those conducting the activity can be monitored whether they are employed by the agency or by a contractor. Measurement of image-building activities is more difficult, since in these activities the emphasis is on changes in attitude, which are difficult to measure. Nevertheless, private firms have found ways of measuring the success of advertising in changing attitudes. Governments can adopt similar techniques.

Three of the government agencies in the sample contracted investment-generating activities. Indonesia's BKPM and Thailand's BOI contracted entire programs to attract investment. Britain's IBB contracted out minor segments of its promotional program.

Indonesia. Beginning in 1984, arrangements were made among the BKPM, USAID, and two consulting firms, Business Advisory Indonesia (BAI) and Resources Management International (RMI), to assist the BKPM in its investment promotion activities. The original contract stipulated that the consulting firms would engage in three separate activities. The first involved preparing feasibility studies or project profiles in specific sectors and packaging these studies so that they could be used in the BKPM's investment missions. The second allowed the firms to provide consulting services to prospective American investors, and Indonesian investors looking for foreign joint-venture partners. The initial contract called for the consultants to provide the first twenty-five hours of consultation to clients interested in investing in Indonesia at no cost to the client. The consulting hours could then be charged to USAID under the investment promotion contract. For the third phase of the project, the consultants were required to coordinate BKPM investment missions to the United States; each firm coordinated a mission to the United States in 1988.

Thailand. Thailand's BOI also subcontracted investment-generating activities, principally to Arthur D. Little, Inc. (ADL), in the United States in 1983, and to several firms, including UNICO & OPMAC, in Japan in 1986. The BOI received additional proposals from private firms to conduct investment-generating activities for the agency. One such proposal, submitted in early 1987 by Coopers & Lybrand, had a cost estimate of close to 50 percent of the BOI's total budget and for that reason was turned down.

The project for U.S. investment promotion consisted of a contract worth $2.2 million with ADL for the provision of investment analysis and promotion services to the BOI and on-the-job training for BOI's New York personnel. ADL, in turn, subcontracted with a New York-based public relations firm, Ruder, Finn, Rotman, and the Thai affiliate of a Philippine firm, SGV-Na Thailand. Activities were subdivided under the contract in the following manner: ADL would be responsible for overall project management, investment planning, opportunity identification, industry and project analysis, and promotion support. Ruder, Finn, Rotman would conduct all investment promotion activities and provide input to investment planning tasks. SGV-Na was responsible for conducting tasks dealing with opportunity identification, local industry analysis, and the provision of promotion support in Thailand. The primary investment-generating activities carried out under the contract were three investment missions to the United States, in the electronics, metal fabricating, and agribusiness sectors.[12]

In 1986, Thailand's BOI again subcontracted investment-generating activities, in this instance to several Japanese and Thai firms to attract Japanese investment, under a $1.5 million contract that consisted primarily of advertising and direct mail activities.

Britain. Britain's IBB was a government agency that, in 1988, was in the process of increasing the extent of its subcontracting. Unlike the subcontracting activities of the BKPM and BOI, however, in which contractors took responsibility for the entire promotional process from initial contact to eventual investment, the IBB contracted out only a segment of an investment-generating program. As foreign direct investment by U.S. firms began to slow, the IBB decided to devote more resources to identification of those companies most likely to invest in Britain. The IBB contracted to economic consultants the process of identifying growth sectors and selling messages for each sector. The next phase of the agency's program, not yet begun in early 1988, was to identify company prospects in each of these growth sectors and prepare briefs on each company. The agency intended to employ consulting firms, accounting firms, or U.S. research firms to prepare the briefs on particular companies, since IBB officials claimed that the organization did not have the resources to conduct this function properly in-house.

Seconding Employees from the Private Sector

An alternative or supplementary technique some government agencies have used to acquire resources and marketing skills that were not available in-house was to obtain employees seconded from the private sector. Two government agencies, Investment Canada and Britain's IBB, obtained employees from the private sector in this way. In both instances selected employees from the private sector were lent to the promotion agencies for several years. The programs were, however, different in a number of respects, including the manner in which these employees were remunerated.

Canada. At the beginning of its second year of operation, after what was perceived by the relevant departments as a successful year of image-building activity, Investment Canada and two other agencies involved to some extent in investment promotion, the Department of Regional and Industrial Expansion (DRIE), and the Department of External Affairs (DEA), decided that future investment promotion activities would be more effective with the input of expertise from the private sector. The agencies decided that senior executives from the private sector or experienced industrial development personnel from throughout Canada should be seconded to Investment Canada/DEA to spearhead promotional efforts at the posts. Six investment counselors were chosen to operate in Canadian embassies or consulates in London, Paris, Bonn, Tokyo, New York, and Los Angeles. The counselors were chosen in a cooperative effort among all three departments. Deputy ministers from Investment Canada, DRIE, and DEA interviewed several possible candidates and agreed upon those considered most suitable.

The six investment counselors were paid from a special industrial development program fund managed by the DEA.

Investment Canada supported the program, since many of the executives at this agency felt that it was important to have marketers with business experience developing personal relations with top executives in foreign corporations. This seemed to be an essential component of successful investment promotion activities.

Britain. Britain's IBB also used employees seconded from the private sector, because the organization explicitly recognized that investment promotion was different from normal government functions and might benefit from private sector participation. Employees came from banks, accounting firms, electronics firms, and others. The IBB had an arrangement with some private British firms to the effect that their employees would be seconded to the IBB for about two years. These employees were usually hired locally by a particular consulate. Since the salaries of locally engaged employees in government organizations were usually lower than salaries that even junior executives received in private companies, the particular private firm made up the difference between the employee's original salary and the salary he received from the local consulate. The companies that participated in this program considered themselves as contributing to the promotion of Britain as an investment site, and they also felt that working with the IBB provided excellent training for selected employees.

Agencies in developing countries and industrial countries differed in several ways. The option of gaining scarce marketing skills by seconding employees from the private to the public sector in Britain and in Canada was possible because of, among other factors, the professionalism and prestige of the civil services in these countries, and the access these agencies, coming from industrial countries, had to a large pool of private sector expertise.[13] The government agencies from developing countries tended, in contrast, to acquire these skills by contracting with private firms. Another difference between these sets of countries was the supply of resources available to conduct the investment promotion function.

Acquiring Resources for Investment Promotion from Abroad

The agencies from the developing countries that we studied had, on the average, fewer resources to conduct the investment promotion function than did the agencies from industrial countries.[14] As a consequence, whatever organizational form the developing countries chose to adopt for investment promotion, whether government, quasi-government, or private, one common characteristic was that, whenever it was possible, the agency initiated efforts to acquire foreign resources and assistance in its investment promotion efforts. Once these resources had been acquired, agencies had to decide how best to use the resources available, especially when they were fungible. Resources and assistance came from the private and public sectors of foreign countries and from multilateral institutions.

Resources from the foreign public sector have come principally from the development assistance organizations of the industrial countries. USAID has fulfilled a particularly significant function in financing investment promotion activities around the world. The manner in which USAID has financed investment promotion operations in the countries that we studied differed with the form of organization used by the country for investment promotion. USAID financed the subcontracting of promotional activities in the government agencies and financed in-house investment promotion activities in the quasi-government and private agencies. The reason for this difference, we suggest, was that the quasi-government and private agencies already had the marketing skills required to conduct investment promotion operations, whereas the government agencies had to initiate an external search for these skills. The extent of USAID involvement in the promotion agencies examined during the course of this research project is summarized in table 9.

Perhaps surprisingly, the USAID offices in each country knew virtually nothing about the support given to promotion efforts by USAID offices elsewhere. There was no attempt to learn from the

for example the Japanese; others put more emphasis on assisting a country's promotional efforts by attracting new investors, for example the Germans.

The German program of resident advisers was probably the most comprehensive. This program was coordinated by the German Finance Company for Investments in Developing Countries (DEG). This organization, funded solely by the German government, provided financial and consulting assistance to German firms interested in investing in developing countries. The DEG offices in the BOI in Thailand and the BKPM in Indonesia had as their principal objectives the matching of small and medium-size German firms with small and medium-size Thai and Indonesian firms. In 1987 DEG was involved in a total of about 400 joint ventures in sixty developing countries.

Investment promotion organizations may also be able to spread their promotional resources further by collaborating with multilateral institutions interested in investment promotion. In 1978 the United Nations Industrial Development Organization (UNIDO) established the Investment Promotion Centre in New York, which offered developing countries the opportunity to conduct U.S. promotional activities out of its offices for a limited time. Between 1978 and 1986, twenty-seven developing countries rented space and operated out of the Centre. UNIDO also operated a center for training investment promotion personnel and had a worldwide investment promotion service, which was headquartered in Vienna.

UNIDO also assisted countries more directly with their investment promotion activities. The agency sponsored and financed a forum in Indonesia in 1987, where 150 foreign businessmen came from around the world to meet with Indonesian businessmen. UNIDO also agreed to finance the training of six Indonesian investment promotion personnel by attaching them to the organization's investment promotion services in Paris, Zurich, Vienna, and Tokyo. In 1988 UNIDO and the BKPM were considering an experiment according to which these persons would be used as traveling promoters once they had completed their training.

The assistance of the foreign private and public sectors and multilateral organizations provided more options for investment promotion agencies, both in the promotional techniques that they could use and in the organizational approaches that they could adopt. This proliferation of options made it even more important that these agencies have some indication of what techniques and what organizational approaches appear to be most effective in attracting foreign direct investment.

In this chapter we have argued that the dominant issue governments face in organizing to promote foreign direct investment is that the investment promotion function resides along a continuum that extends from traditional government organization to wholly private sector organization. The empirical evidence suggests that the position of the investment promotion organization along this continuum, whether government, quasi-government, or private, is an important factor in explaining the patterns with which investment promotion organizations gain access to marketing skills that are often available only in the private sector, the ability of these agencies to conduct tasks normally associated with government organizations, such as service to investors, and the manner in which they conduct overseas marketing. The choice even has an effect on the kind of foreign assistance they are likely to receive. In the following chapter we shall report our findings on the relative effectiveness of these organizational approaches.

Notes

1. See, for example, Dennis J. Encarnation and Louis T. Wells, Jr. "Sovereignty en Garde: Negotiating with Foreign Investors," *International Organization* 39 (Winter 1985); Sanjaya Lall and Paul Streeten, *Foreign Investment, Transnationals and Developing Countries* (Boulder, Colo.: Westview Press, 1977); and J. de la Torre, "Foreign Investment and Economic Development: Conflict and Negotiation," *Journal of International Business Studies*, Fall 1981, pp. 9–32.

2. This hypothesis is drawn from the work of Encarnation and Wells. They discuss the political costs of adopting coordinated and centralized structures for negotiations with investors, but they also point out that these structures are likely to lead to greater promotion of investment opportunities than dispersed structures. See Encarnation and Wells, "Sovereignty En Garde," pp.58, 76–77.

3. Investment promotion exhibits two of the characteristics Robinson identifies as reasons for the existence of public sector enterprise—the inability to internalize profit, the tendency to monopoly, the need for pioneer industry, the inadequacy of private resources; the need for public revenue with which to finance, the need for public control, and high risk caused by uncertainty with respect to the timing and amount of payout from the investment. See Richard Robinson, "Major Issues in Joint Ventures between Developed and Developing Countries," in *Joint Ventures and Public Enterprises in Developing Countries,* ed. V. V. Ramanadham (Ljubljana, Yugoslavia: International Center for Public Enterprises in Developing Countries, 1980). It is virtually impossible to internalize profit from investment promotion activities, so these activities have to be financed from public revenue.

4. See, for example. Claudio Alhaique, *Creation of an Industrial Promotion Service* (Paris: OECD, 1972). In his recommendations for creating an industrial promotion service he states, "The Service should enjoy the maximum possible operational autonomy and flexibility, which is why it is not advisable to insert it directly in the government apparatus, but to find the legal form required to guarantee these features" (p. 50). A more recent recommendation with respect to institutional support for export promotion is that it is probably best to keep export promotion partly outside the official sphere during transitional stages, while export climates are being improved, and when it has been made official, to ensure that such an organization has a semi-independent status, with its own board of directors consisting primarily of people from the export community. See Donald B. Keesing, "Marketing Manufactured Exports From Developing Countries: How to Provide Excellent. Cost-Effective Institutional Support" (World Bank: Country Economics Department—Trade Policy Division: April 1988) p. 43, 14 (appendix).

5. These regulations were regularly pointed to by both the international and domestic business communities as obstacles to investment. Although the international investment community in Malaysia supported the objectives of the NEP, it was also concerned about the numerous regulations that had been created in the setting of the NEP that made business operations in Malaysia fraught with the problems of complying with government regulations. For a sample of the concerns of the international business community, see 'View of Foreign Investors: A Contribution to the Preparation of the Fifth Malaysia Plan," Kuala Lumpur: Malaysian International Chamber of Commerce & Industry. 1985.

6. The experiments with privatization that have received the most attention have been those carried out by the Thatcher government in Great Britain. For a review of British experiences with privatization. see Madsen Pine, *Privitization in Theory and Practice* (London: ASI Research Ltd., 1985) for the views from a proponent of privatization; and Paul Starr, "The Limits of Privatization." in *Prospects for Privatization,* ed. Steve H. Hanke, (Montpelier, Vermont: Capital City Press, 1987), for a rebuttal.

7. Empirical observations from current research suggest that investment promotion is best conducted by individuals and organizations that have primary responsibility for this activity. In countries that housed the investment promotion function with another function such as exports—in Chile, Argentina, and Spain, for example—it appeared that most resources were spent on export promotion; for these countries, resources spent on investment promotion varied from about 5 to 10 percent of the organization's resources. Further, any investment promotion that was done tended to be passive rather than active Similarly, empirical observations from other studies suggest that export promotion suffers when coupled with investment promotion; see Keesing, "Marketing Manufactured Exports from Developing Countries," p26.

8. This is not to say, however, that the promotion agency cannot bring some expertise to a collaborative effort with the professional firm. It is likely that many agencies work closely with professional firms. In this research at least two instances of close collaboration were identified. In the cases of both Ireland's IDA and Israel's Investment Authority, these

organizations were able to work very closely with advertising agencies. IDA worked closely with its advertising agency in producing the advertising theme, "We're the Young Europeans." Israel's Investment Authority did most of the writing for the advertising supplements it produced and worked closely with its advertising firm in the design of several advertisements geared to promoting Israel as a high-technology center.

9. See Pine, *Privatization in Theory and Practice,* for a discussion of several aspects of privatization. Pine points out that since 1979 the British government has used twenty-two different methods of transferring public operations, of which contracting activities to the private sector is one, wholly or in part into the private sector.

10. Some estimates put the reduction in costs from contracting out government services at 20 to 50 percent. See Stephen Moore, "Contracting Out: A Painless Alternative to the Budget Cutter's Knife," in *Prospects for Privatization,* ed. Hanke. p. 61. Moore also emphasizes that contracting out provides the government organization with greater access to expertise.

11. A voluminous literature on SOEs in general and performance evaluation of SOEs in particular has emerged. The literature on performance evaluation incorporates the following works: Leroy Jones, "Towards a Performance Evaluation Methodology for Public Enterprise: With Special Reference to Pakistan," in *International Symposium on Economic Performance of Public Enterprise* (Islamabad, Pakistan: United Nations Department of Technical Cooperation for Development, Nov. 1981); R. Mallon, "Performance Evaluation and Compensation of the Social Burdens of Public Enterprises in Less Developed Countries," *Annals of Public and Cooperative Economy* 52 (1981); and Mary M. Shirley. *Managing State-Owned Enterprises.* Staff Working Papers no. 577 (Washington, D.C.: World Bank, 1983). See Robert Bailey, "Uses and Misuses of Privatization," in *Prospects for Privatization.* ed. Hanke, pp. 148–49, for a discussion of the importance of establishing monitoring units within public agencies to evaluate contract compliance.

12. Details of the objectives of the contract and the activities it stipulates are formally listed in Donald J. Rhatigan and Associates, "Final Evalu-

ation of Private Sector in Development," (Washington, D.C.: TVT Associates, July 1987).

13. The civil services of many countries differ significantly in their prestige. Aharoni points out that in many countries a career in the public sector is considered respectable and carries high status, attracting the best-educated people in the society, whereas in others employment in the public sector, except in the top positions, is regarded as a secondclass occupation, and the remuneration is poor. These differences are likely to affect the need for government organizations to acquire private sector expertise, and their ability to attract this expertise. See Yair Aharoni. *Markets, Planning and Development: The Private and Public Sectors in Economic Development* (Cambridge, MA: Ballinger Publishing Co.. 1978), pp. 286–87.

14. We estimate, on the basis of incomplete data, that the budgets of the agencies from developing countries averaged to US$4.5 million in 1986, and the budgets of the agencies from industrial countries averaged to $12.6 million in 1986. These estimates are imprecise, however, because no agency provided a detailed analysis of resources expended solely on the promotion of foreign direct investment. Further, in many instances, especially those in which the government organizations were concerned, there were many problems in estimating expenses incurred by consulates and embassies in promoting investment. We do not feel that this imprecision affects our basic point, however, that industrial countries spend far more on promoting investment than do developing countries.

4

Evaluating the Investment Promotion Function

After developing investment promotion strategies that are based, in part, on the parallels between investment promotion and industrial marketing and adopting structures that can handle both the public and the private tasks that make up the investment promotion function, agencies still face the important task of evaluating the effectiveness of their promotion efforts. Evaluations are often important in justifying budgets to the government. They are necessary if the agency is to learn from its experience so that it can allocate its funds more efficiently among different types of activity. Evaluation is also essential if work is to be contracted to others. Although evaluation is of the utmost importance, it is one of the most difficult tasks facing a promotion agency. The ways in which the agencies we studied undertook this task differed considerably. Approaches to evaluation differed according to whether the agency was emphasizing image building, investment generation, or investment service.

Several evaluations of the effectiveness of these various kinds of promotion activity and of the efforts of government and quasi-government organizational structures were either discovered or conducted during this research. These attempts at evaluation are particularly instructive in discovering the types of activity and structure that promote investment most effectively.

The Evaluation Processes Used by Investment Promotion Agencies

Investment promotion agencies tend to evaluate image-building and investment-service activities on an ad hoc basis. The process of evaluating these activities is rarely integrated into the management control system of the agency. On the other hand, investment-generating activities, when conducted in-house, tend to be evaluated continuously with an evaluation process that is highly integrated into the control system of the agency. The evaluation processes typical of the different types of investment promotion activity are summarized in table 10.

Evaluation Processes for Image Building and Investment Service

Evaluations of image-building and investment-service activities are conducted infrequently, if at all, and the evaluations that are con-

Table 10. Evaluation of Investment Promotion by Type of Activity

Promotional activity	Typical evaluation process
Image building	Ad hoc, project-based evaluations. Evaluation not integrated into management control system of agency. Evaluation conducted by external organization.
Investment service	Similar to process for image building.
Investment-generating activities conducted in-house	Continuous process of evaluation. Evaluations performed by agency and evaluation process highly integrated into management control system of agency.
Investment-generating activities contracted out	Evaluation conducted on a project basis by contractor or by independent evaluator hired by organization financing activity. Evaluation process process not integrated into management control system of contractor or of agency.

ducted are performed by external organizations and not by the promotion agency itself. In their evaluations of image-building activities, external organizations have relied on measurements of changes in the attitudes of the target population after the promotion campaigns have been conducted.

Most agencies, however, have neither arranged for external organizations to conduct evaluations of their image-building activities, nor evaluated these activities themselves. This is especially true of the relatively low cost activities such as missions and seminars. There were no indications that any agency had attempted to evaluate these activities according to their potential to change or build images. A few agencies attempted to evaluate these activities in terms of their ability to generate investment. The results suggested that these activities were consistently ineffective in generating investment.

Agencies that have attempted to build image through advertising campaigns have faced the greatest pressure to evaluate the effectiveness of their image-building activity because of the high cost of advertising. Evaluations of advertising activities were conducted by the Canadian Conference Board for Investment Canada, by *Business Week* for Ireland's IDA, Scotland's LIS, and Britain's IBB, by the Japanese consulting firm UNICO & OPMAC for Thailand's BOI, and by the U.S. market research firm Louis Harris and Associates, Inc., for IDA.

Several evaluations of the effectiveness of these various kinds of promotion activity and of the efforts of government and quasi-government organizational structures were either discovered or conducted during this research. These attempts at evaluation are particularly instructive in discovering the types of activity and structure that promote investment most effectively.[1]

Evaluation Process for Investment-Generating Activities

Some agencies adopted a different process for evaluating investment-generating activities from those used for evaluating image-building and investment-service activities. Agencies that performed investment-generating activities in-house adopted an internal evaluation process for these activities that was highly integrated into the agency's management control system. Agencies that contracted out investment-generating activities, however, used an evaluation process similar to the one used to evaluate image-building and investment-service activities, relying on infrequent evaluations by third parties or the contractors.

Investment promotion agencies that conducted investment-generating activities in-house generally operated under the assumption that the personal selling activities of individual promotion officials could be tied to actual investments if a comprehensive information and tracking system was put in place to accomplish this objective. These agencies also unanimously regarded personal interactions between an investment promoter and a prospective investor as the most effective approach to promotion. The control systems developed by these agencies were simultaneously useful in informing management about the investment-generating activities of each member of the marketing team, allowing for the evaluation and control of these persons, and providing a basis for motivating overseas marketers to increase their levels of productivity.

All the promotion agencies in the sample that conducted investment-generating activities in-house, whether the agencies were government, quasi-government, or private, attempted to develop integrated control systems that included an evaluation component. Some of the quasi-government and private agencies also built financial incentives for overseas marketers into their control systems.

Evaluation Process for In-house Promotion. The management control systems employed by Costa Rica's CINDE, Ireland's IDA, and Scotland's LIS illustrated the level of integration of systems in agencies that conducted investment-generating activities in-house and emphasized personal selling. Within CINDE, the performance of employees, especially overseas marketing staff, was evaluated by a management-by-objectives system. Each overseas promotion official was expected to make twenty sales presentations a month, to generate fifteen site visits by potential investors a year, and to generate each year approved investment that would employ 750 people. These activities were to be within industries that had been targeted by CINDE. Promotion officials operated within a set of assumptions about yields, which differed by sector. The average expectation was that every ten contacts would yield one appointment, ten presentations at appointments would yield one site visit, and ten site visits would yield one investment. Bonuses were paid to CINDE's overseas promotion staff for jobs attracted in excess of the target of 750 jobs a year. These bonuses could equal as much as 13 percent of an employee's base salary.

This evaluation system was integrated with an information system for reporting and tracking results. Each overseas promotion official submitted a monthly activity report, in which the number of sales presentations, the number of site visits, the number of projects in the pipeline, the number of projects approved, and the number of jobs approved were indicated. The probability of realization for each project, and the associated jobs were also included. The assignment of probabilities allowed CINDE to calculate the expected value of incoming projects and jobs.

The IDA management control system was similar to CINDE's— not surprising, since the CINDE system was patterned after IDA's. Overseas officers had targets for the number of sales presentations, number of site visits generated, and number of approved jobs they should attract. The agency's Dublin staff had targets for the number of approved jobs and number of jobs actually created. In evaluating overseas officers the IDA management was concerned, not only with the number of sales presentations, but also with the level of management to which these presentations were given, since the prevailing view within the agency was that presentations given to an audience of senior managers were more likely to have an effect on a firm's investment decision than presentations that were not attended by senior managers. Above-average performers within the IDA system could receive financial bonuses of 3–4 percent of their base salaries. In the case of Scotland's LIS, which also had a similar motivation, evaluation, and control system, the best-performing overseas representatives could earn an additional 20 percent of their base salaries in financial bonuses.

Evaluation Process for Contracted Promotional Activities. In contrast to the evaluation process for investment-generating activities that were conducted in-house, investment-generating activities that were contracted to external organizations were evaluated independent of the promotional organization. Promotion agencies relied either on evaluations conducted by the contractor or on evaluations conducted by another external organization. Evaluations, even those made by contractors, were usually conducted on a project basis rather than on a continuous basis. The contractors, regarding the promotional activity as short-term and separate from their normal business functions, did not integrate the evaluation process into the management control systems of their organizations.

The investment promotion activities contracted out by Thailand's BOI and Indonesia's BKPM were all evaluated by third parties. The BOI's promotional activities in the United States, contracted to Arthur D. Little, Inc., were independently evaluated by economic consultant Donald Rhatigan. The agency's investment promotion activities in Japan, which were contracted to the Japanese firm UNICO & OPMAC, were evaluated by that firm. The BKPM's investment promotion activities that were contracted, with financing by USAID, to two consulting firms, Business Advisory Indonesia and Resources Management International, were evaluated midway through the term of the contract by USAID. The evaluations were based solely on data submitted by the consulting firms. In early 1988, there were no plans by USAID or the BKPM to evaluate the performance of the contractors when the contracts expired at the end of that year.

Our observations suggest that the characteristic that distinguishes the process by which different promotional techniques and strategies are evaluated is the degree to which the process is integrated into the management control system of an agency. On the one hand, image-building, investment-service, and investment-generating activities contracted to an external organization were not evaluated in the course of the agency's regular operations. As a consequence, evaluations of these activities were conducted sporadically, if at all. On the other hand, agencies that conducted investment-generating activities in-house made attempts to develop integrated control systems that included an evaluation component.

The Effectiveness of Investment Promotion

Although we were unable to obtain systematic evaluations of all types of promotional activities and structures, those that were available, coupled with the ones we made, gave some indication of the promotional techniques and structures that were most effective in attracting foreign direct investment.

A Statistical Test. Before we report the results of various efforts to measure the effectiveness of particular investment promotion techniques and structures, we shall present the results of an attempt to determine, with aggregate data, whether investment promotion seems to make any difference in the overall flows of foreign investment. Such aggregate studies, we believe, should be taken with a healthy grain of salt. Nevertheless, when the results are consistent with the findings of others, they are likely to be indicative of general patterns. This analysis, as indicated in chapter 1, at least suggests that promotion might have a significant influence on foreign investment flows.

According to Agarwal, "foreign direct investment has registered an enormous growth over the past three decades [until 1980]. The growth of foreign direct investment has, however, been excelled by the growth of publications specially on the determinants of these investments."[2] The numerous attempts to isolate the determinants of foreign direct investment that have been made would seem to make another such study unnecessary. Indeed, we make no claim that in the study reported in this section a new, comprehensive model that explains the determinants of foreign direct investment has been developed. Such an activity would be an unnecessary drain of society's resources, particularly the reader's time. Instead, we shall seek to build on the existing knowledge to examine a phenomenon that has been totally ignored in this literature. Despite the fact that many countries have engaged in explicit marketing efforts to attract foreign direct investors to their shores, in no existing study of the determinants of foreign direct investment have these activities been taken into account as a possible determinant of this investment. Thus, we shall take these activities into account by adding investment promotion to a multiple regression model that includes other variables that have seemed in earlier studies to have a statistically significant relation to foreign direct investment.

The dependent variable, foreign direct investment, is measured by per capita foreign direct investment flows,[3] as in several other empirical studies on the determinants of foreign direct investment.[4] As in these studies, we do not include additions to existing foreign direct investment through retained earnings. It would be possible, in fact, to argue both for and against the inclusion of retained earnings. For many countries, however, the data required to include retained earnings simply do not exist.

Researchers have examined political, economic, social, and policy variables in attempts to isolate those that seem to be most important.[5] We shall draw from the findings of their studies.

Several researchers have tested proxies of market demand levels and market growth rates of host economies to see whether there is a statistical association between these proxies and inflows of foreign direct investment. In general, most have found evidence of a statistical association. John H. Dunning, for example, suggested that one of the dominant influences on foreign direct investment was the growth and size of the host country market.[6] Root and Ahmed and Schneider and Frey found statistically significant relation between foreign direct investment and market demand (as measured by per capita GDP or GNP) and market growth (as measured by the growth rate of GDP or GNP).

We also included measures of market demand in this study. Following Schneider and Frey, we used GNP per capita. Our hypothesis was that the higher the per capita income, the greater the per capita foreign investment inflow.[7] Accordingly, the expected sign of this variable is positive. Our hypothesis with respect to the growth rate of the market was that the higher the rate of economic growth, the greater the investment inflows.[8] In this as in other variables, causality could, of course, run in either or both directions. Foreign investors could be attracted by high growth rates, and high growth rates could be the result of foreign investment.

Schneider and Frey found a statistically significant relation between inflation rates and foreign direct investment, as well as between current account positions and foreign direct investment.[9] Other researchers also found statistically significant relations for these variables.[10] We therefore hypothesized that foreign investors would be deterred by a high rate of inflation and by unfavorable current accounts in a country's balance of payments.[11]

Several researchers have tested the influence of political stability or, conversely, political risk, on foreign direct investment flows. Early survey studies of the foreign investment decision process indicated that political instability was one of the main factors in the decisions of investors not to invest in a particular country. Both Basi and Aharoni concluded from their research that, after market size and growth, political instability was the dominant influence on investment flows.[12] In a study conducted by Root and Ahmed, political stability was one of the variables that was found to be statistically significant.[13] Levis concluded that political stability, although, unlike economic factors, not the prime determinant of foreign direct investment, was nevertheless an important determinant of investment.[14]

This study includes a political stability variable, which is based on Frost & Sullivan's 1984 forecast of political risk in eighty countries.[15] The hypothesis is that the more politically stable the country, the greater the inflows of foreign direct investment.

Investment promotion is the one new variable that we include in a regression model.[16] To some extent, the other variables represent controls for a test on the promotion variable. Although in some studies, such as Root and Ahmed's,[17] some policy variables have been included, no studies have included a variable to measure whether or not a country engages in marketing activities designed to attract investment.

The variables to be included in the model, the measures to be used, and the hypothesized signs are summarized in table 11. The countries used in this model are listed in table 12.

Researchers have used a variety of statistical methodologies to test various versions of models designed to explain foreign direct investment flows. These include multiple discriminant analysis and multiple regression analysis, including stepwise regression.[18] In this study we used multiple regression techniques, since continuous, rather than categorical, variables were used to measure foreign di-

Table 11. Model of the Determinants of Foreign Direct Investment

Variable	Proxy	Hypothesized sign
Dependent variable		
Foreign direct investment	Foreign direct investment per capita	+
Independent variables		
Effective demand	Per capita GNP	+
Market growth	GNP growth rate	+
Balance of payments condition	BOP current account balance	−
Inflation	Annual rate of inflation	−
Political stability	Frost & Sullivan's political stability index	+
Investment promotion	*Business Facilities'* listing of countries actively promoting in the United States (promotion = 1)	+

Note: Analysis of the model: The model was tested on a data set of 50 industrial and developing countries for which all the above variables were available. The countries are listed in table 12.

Table 12. Data Set of Industrial and Developing Countries

Industrial countries	Developing countries
Australia	Argentina
Austria	Bolivia
Belgium	Brazil
Canada	Cameroon
Denmark	Chile
Finland	Colombia
France	Costa Rica
Federal Republic of Germany	Dominican Republic
Greece	Ecuador
Ireland	Egypt
Italy	El Salvador
Japan	Guatemala
Netherlands	Honduras
New Zealand	Indonesia
Portugal	Israel
Spain	Jamaica
Sweden	Kenya
United Kingdom	Republic of Korea
	Malaysia
	Mexico
	Morocco
	Nigeria
	Pakistan
	Panama
	Philippines
	Singapore
	Sri Lanka
	Thailand
	Tunisia
	Turkey
	Venezuela
	Zaire

rect investment flows. Since the variables included had all been identified as significant in the literature—except, of course, the promotion variable—there was no need to employ techniques such as stepwise regression to select potential variables.

The investment, GNP per capita, and inflation variables were transformed to their logarithmic equivalents, since a preliminary analysis showed that several variables had skewed process distributions. After the transformations, these variables had distributions that were nearly normal.[19] The results of the multiple regression on the full data set are shown in table 13.

Tests of the model on the full data set indicated that the entire model had relatively high explanatory power $(R^2 = 70.26$ percent). All the variables had the hypothesized signs, although the growth, deficit, and inflation variables were not statistically significant. The GNP per capita variable was statistically significant at the 5 percent level, however and the variables for political stability and investment promotion were statistically significant at better than the 1 percent level The promotion variable offered the highest individual contribution to R^2, 15 percent.[20] Also, the standardized coefficient of the promotion variable was larger than the others, indicating that this variable had the greatest effect on foreign direct investment flows.

As a further test of the model, the data on industrial and developing countries were separated to test whether the regres-

Table 13. Results of Multiple Regression—Analysis on the Full Data Set

Variable	Beta coefficient[a]	Standard error	Probability[b]
Constant	0.000	0.082	0.042
LogGNP	0.240[c]	0.126	0.032
Growth	0.047	0.960	0.313
Deficit	−0.071	0.092	0.220
LogInflation	−0.063	0.092	0.249
Stability	0.335[d]	0.124	0.005
Promotion	0.453[d]	0.095	0.000

Note: Dependent variable: LogInvest. $R^2 = 0.7026$; F=17.3(6,44); $P = 0$.

a. The coefficients used were the beta, or unconditionally standardized, coefficients, which, unlike natural coefficients, are independent of the unite of measurement.

b. The probability listed in the regression tables as the probability that the true sign of the variable is opposite to that shown in the regression table.

c. Statistically significant at the 5 percent level.

d. Statistically significant at the 1 percent level.

sion on the pooled data was masking major dissimilarities be-tween these two groups of countries. Some researchers have suggested that studies that do not treat industrial and develop-ing countries differently are methodologically deficient, because different factors are likely to determine the level of foreign in-vestment inflows in these two groups.[21] Further, in this research we found differences in the promotional activities of industrial and developing countries. Table 14 records the results obtained from multiple regressions run on the set of eighteen industrial countries.

For this set of countries, the explanatory power of the model was again quite high, with an R^2 of 68 percent. The inflation and deficit variables, however, did not have the expected signs. Fur-ther, these variables plus the GNP per capita, and stability variables were statistically insignificant at the 5 percent level. The statisti-cally significant variables were growth (5 percent level) and pro-motion (1 percent level). For this set of countries, promotion again offered the highest individual contribution to the R^2, 40 percent, and the largest effect on foreign direct investment.

Regressions were also run on the data set of developing coun-tries to test for the influence of promotion; see table 15 for the results.

Table 14. Results of Multiple Regression Analysis on the Set of Industrial Countries

Variable	Beta coefficient	Standard error	Probability
Constant	0.000	0.156	0.000
LogGNP	0.120	0.246	0.318
Growth	0.439[a]	0.286	0.074
Deficit	0.216	0.288	0.234
LogInflation	0.186	0.293	0.269
Stability	0.330	0.249	0.104
Promotion	0.818[b]	0.195	0.001

Note: Dependent variable: LogInvest. $R^2 = 0.6852$; $F = 9.35(6,12)$; $P = 0$.
a. Statistically significant at the 5 percent level.
b. Statistically significant at the 1 percent level.

Table 15. Results of Multiple Regression Analysis on the Set of Developing Countries

Variable	Beta coefficient	Standard error	Probability
Constant	0.000	0.132	0.000
LogGNP	0.381[a]	0.154	0.010
Growth	−0.026	0.165	0.439
Deficit	−0.174	0.154	0.135
LogInflation	−0.103	0.134	0.225
Stability	0.380[a]	0.153	0.010
Promotion	0.297[b]	0.154	0.034

Note: Dependent variable: LogInvest. $R^2 = 0.5809$; $F = 5.54(6,26)$; $P = 0.001$.
a. Statistically significant at the 1 percent level.
b. Statistically significant at the 5 percent level

The results show that GNP per capita, inflation, deficit, stability and promotion variables all had the expected signs. The growth variable did not have the expected sign, suggesting that this variable might be a less important determinant of foreign investment in developing countries than in industrial countries.[22] The R^2 was 58 percent; the promotion variable made the third highest contribution, 6.4 percent, to this figure. The highest contributions came from the per capita GNP and stability variables, each contributing about 11 percent.

Although all three analyses suggested that the investment promotion variable had a statistically significant relationship with inflows of foreign direct investment, there was a relatively large difference between the influence of promotion in industrial countries and the influence of this variable in developing countries. In the sample of industrial countries, promotion was the most significant variable, whereas in the sample of developing countries the income and political stability variables were more important. This finding can perhaps be explained by the fact that promotion is likely to have the largest effect where other factors that attract investment—product factors such as income levels and degrees of political stability, for example—are most similar, as is true of industrial countries. In developing countries, where there is a greater diversity in the product factors, the effect of promotion is subordinated to the effects of these other factors.

Additional tests were conducted to verify that the model was properly specified, including tests for the existence of heteroskedasticity, undue influence of isolated variables, autocorrelation, and multicollinearity.[23] The tests suggested that the model had been properly specified and that, accordingly, it provided reasonable estimates.

We cannot, with these data, prove that causality runs from promotion to investment; nevertheless, it seems unlikely that increases in foreign investment will typically cause increases in promotion. Less certain are the influences of variables that are not included. It may be that countries that actively promote investment do other things well that attract foreign investors. They may offer more attractive tax incentives, for example.[24] Nevertheless, the analysis does provide a strong hint that promotion might influence investment flows. Evaluations of particular promotional techniques (such as image building, investment service, and investment generation, and of different structures, such as government and quasi-government) add considerably to the evidence on the influence of promotion on investment flows and to an understanding of the kinds of investors likely to be influenced by promotion efforts.

Effectiveness of Image-Building Activities

In evaluations of image-building activities an attempt to measure the effectiveness of advertising is usually made. The evaluations are not always systematic, however.

Several agencies acquired anecdotal evidence to suggest that their advertisements generated widespread readership. The results of surveys by Starch Inra Hooper, a U.S. marketing firm, for example, were cited by Ireland's IDA. This firm performed regular "STARCH" surveys of advertisements appearing in *Business Week* to generate estimates of advertisement recall by *Business Week* readers. In 1986 an advertisement of Ireland's IDA that appeared in this publication received the *Business Week* "Starch Excellence Award" for the best-read advertisement ever recorded in the area development category. During the period 1985–87 the agency's advertisements were also regularly among the top three or four recalled by *Business Week* readers, including advertisements for consumer products. In 1986 the Scottish Development Administration (SDA)—parent organization for Locate in Scotland—also received a Starch Excellence Award to honor its outstanding performance in measures of advertising recall by *Business Week* readers.

Some agencies turned to general evaluations of their country's investment climate as indicators of the effectiveness of their image-building campaigns, including the advertising component of these campaigns. Two such agencies were Investment Canada and Jamaica's JNIP.

In the wake of Investment Canada's image-building campaign, the Canadian Conference Board surveyed investors to ascertain Canada's image as an investment location. The results suggested that investors had a positive image of Canada. Similarly, in the fall of 1983, the U.S. Business Committee on Jamaica conducted a survey of investors' attitudes toward investing in Jamaica, from which they found that "Jamaica has done a superb job of changing its image from one viewed as hostile to private investment to one viewed as friendly to it."[25] Investment Canada and the JNIP used these evaluations to suggest that their image-building campaigns had been effective. In both situations, however, the evaluations took place in the aftermath of changes to probusiness, conservative governments. Also, in neither situation was there a benchmark survey of precampaign attitudes with which the postcampaign survey results could be compared. The lessons from research in corporate advertising suggest that evaluations of image-building activities are most useful when both precampaign and postcampaign measures of the attitudes of the target population are used.[26]

Ireland. One agency, Ireland's IDA, did use precampaign data on attitudes. The IDA regularly advertised and systematically assessed the effectiveness of its advertising in building the desired images. During the 1980s, IDA subcontracted evaluation of its advertising program to Louis Harris and Associates, Inc. The regular evaluation exercise included pre- and post-measures of the attitudes of the target population. The Lou Harris survey covered not only the perceptions of investors but also factual recall of the advertisements, a technique that many in advertising circles use as an indicator of the effectiveness of advertising.[27]

One such survey was conducted in 1982. In that year, the Lou Harris survey of prospective investors—the precampaign measure of attitudes—indicated that investors still perceived Ireland as a source of low-cost and low-skilled labor. By this time, Ireland had realized that it could no longer compete in the market for internationally mobile investment on a cost basis only and had spent the previous years investing in education. By 1982 the level of education of the Irish work force had increased considerably. The 1982 survey, coupled with the improvements in the education of the work force, suggested that there was a need to change investors' perceptions—now misperceptions—about the Irish work force. This was the motivation for the IDA to begin its advertising campaign around the theme "We're the Young Europeans."

Another Lou Harris survey was conducted in October and November 1986, after the advertising campaign had been running for three years, generating the postcampaign measure of attitudes. The firm conducted a telephone survey among corporate executives and decisionmakers responsible for selecting overseas manufacturing locations in five industries: consumer products, health care, engineering, electronics, and computers. One hundred fifty interviews were completed, with thirty respondents from each of the five industries. The survey focused on investors' perceptions of the labor forces of various Western European countries, and included questions designed to assess the efficacy of the advertising programs of these countries. The results of the survey provided no evidence that perceptions of the quality of the Irish labor force had changed significantly. The communication skills of the labor force were seen as the republic's best asset, but the investors surveyed felt that the country was still short on technical skills. The survey did, however, provide much evidence to the effect that senior decisionmakers in U.S. corporations saw investment promotion advertisements in general, read the IDA's advertisements, and remembered these advertisements, including the theme of the advertisements.

The corporate executives surveyed were asked the following question: "Some countries in Western Europe advertise in leading business magazines, trying to tell people like yourself about the attractions of the country and to persuade you to consider locating a plant there. Can you remember seeing any advertisements like this?" Out of the one hundred fifty executives surveyed, ninety remembered seeing this type of advertisement and were asked several other questions.

They were first asked: "Which countries in Western Europe can you remember being advertised in this way?" (without any specific countries mentioned). The second: "Which of the following countries, if any, can you remember advertising in this way?" (specific countries were mentioned). And finally: "One country's advertising concentrates on the quality of its people, its young population, and the high standards of its education system. Can you remember which country advertises this way?" The responses to these questions are listed in tables 16, 17, and 18.

The IDA and Louis Harris and Associates, Inc., concluded from the survey, on the basis of the high measures of recall, that the agency's advertising program was effective but that more time was needed for the advertising to change investors' images of the Irish labor force. Accordingly, the IDA continued to run the same advertising program after the 1986 survey.

This research uncovered only one instance in which evaluations of image-building activities seemed to indicate that these activities had been successful in generating investment directly. This was the special marketing program sponsored by Thailand's BOI in Japan.

Table 16. Recall of Investment Promotion Advertisements of Western European Countries
(List of Countries Not Supplied)

Country	First mention (percent)	Also mentioned[a] (percent)
Republic of Ireland	39	8
Britain (Northern Ireland)	22	16
Britain (England)	16	13
Holland (Netherlands)	3	12
France	3	1
Germany, Fed. Rep.	3	15
Spain	3	12
Scotland	3	13
Other	3	4
None	2	11
Not sure	5	11

a. Percentages for this category do not add to 100 percent because multiple responses were allowed.

Source: Louis Harris and Associates, Inc., *European Locations Survey,* 1986

Table 17. Recall of Investment Promotion Advertisements of Western European Countries
(With Specific Countries Mentioned)

Country	Total[a] (percent)
Republic of Ireland	66
Britain (Northern Ireland)	50
Britain (England)	46
Scotland	37
Germany, Fed. Rep.	32
Spain	25
Holland (Netherlands)	24
France	15

a. Multiple responses allowed.

Source: Louis Harris and Associates, Inc., *European Locations Survey,* 1986

Table 18. Testing the Recall of the IDA's Advertising Theme

Country	First mention (percent)	Also mentioned (percent)
Republic of Ireland	26	9
Britain (Northern Ireland)	14	5
Holland (Netherlands)	8	1
Germany, Fed. Rep.	6	1
Britain (England)	5	2
Scotland	5	3
Spain	—	3
France	—	3
Other	1	2
None	7	31

Source: Louis Harris and Associates, Inc., European Locations Survey, 1986.

Thailand. The Thai government that came to power in 1986 wanted to increase the rate of economic growth in Thailand. It allocated total funds of about $61 million for its economic recovery program. Each government department was eligible to submit a budget requesting an appropriation of funds for a one-time project that would help in the process of economic recovery. The BOI submitted a request for about $2 million to attract foreign direct investment.

The bulk of this additional budget, about $1.5 million, was used to mount an advertising campaign and a direct mail campaign in Japan. Contracts were made with several firms, including UNICO & OPMAC, to do the direct mailings, beginning with an initial list of 6,000 firms, and to process the anticipated responses from the advertisements and mailings. A Thai consulting firm, Industrial Management Company, Ltd., was engaged to do background research in Thailand to provide the information required to respond to requests from prospective investors. Two firms, a Japanese firm, Synergy, in collaboration with a Thai firm, Meitsu, were engaged to develop the advertising copy and carry out the advertising campaign in Japanese media.

The advertisements were placed in sixteen leading Japanese daily newspapers, primarily general financial media. Most of the advertisements carried coupons, and they specified preferred sectors for investment. The advertisements directed the reader to return coupons with requests for information to UNICO & OPMAC, the Japanese consulting firm. These advertisements generated significant numbers of responses. The first advertisement alone generated 117 responses, and about 500 companies submitted requests for more information on Thailand with each running of the campaign.[28]

The primary study of the effectiveness of the promotional campaign came from evaluations conducted by UNICO & OPMAC in 1987. In the aftermath of the campaign, the firm surveyed a sample of investors who had recently invested or were considering investing in Thailand. The survey results suggested that about half the firms had developed their initial interest from the advertising campaign. In their evaluation of the effectiveness of the total promotional effort, which included the direct mail campaign and its follow-up, the consulting company also indicated that eighty companies that made site visits to Thailand in the wake of the promotional effort had been approached by them or had asked them for information. Of these eighty site visits, thirteen had led to investment applications, and sixty investors were still conducting feasibility studies at the time of the evaluation.

Even taking into account the possible bias in the measure of effectiveness because the evaluation was conducted by an organization that participated in the promotional effort, there is ample evidence that in this instance the advertisements in general financial media created immediate interest and eventual investment. The responses received suggest that the advertisements did much more than build or change images.

This single instance hardly demonstrates that advertising in general financial media can routinely be expected to generate investment directly, especially in the light of the numerous experiences of other agencies that have found such activities ineffective in generating investment. In fact, drawing conclusions about the effectiveness of this particular advertising campaign is also made difficult by the fact that the advertising campaign was coupled with a direct mail campaign conducted by UNICO & OPMAC. Indeed, the weight of the empirical evidence indicates that advertising cannot be routinely used to generate investment.

Nevertheless, the anomaly needs an explanation. One possible hypothesis to explain the apparent success of the BOI's campaign is that the advertising program generated unexpected results because it coincided with atypical, significant interest on the part of the Japanese in investing in low-wage ASEAN countries. The rapid appreciation in the Japanese yen during the period 1985–87 provided a strong impetus for Japanese firms to locate manufacturing abroad to keep the costs of their exports, particularly to the United States market, competitive. Countries that could be expected to benefit from this impetus were relatively low-wage ASEAN countries, such as Thailand, Malaysia, and Indonesia. That there was increased investment interest in these countries from Japanese investors during this period is demonstrated by an examination of the investment applications and approvals in these countries during the same period. Although Thailand saw increases in the proportion of investment applications and approvals coming from Japan during 1986 and 1987, when the campaign was conducted, Malaysia and Indonesia also saw significant increases during that same period (see table 19).

This evidence suggests that the already substantially increasing and atypical interest on the part of the Japanese in investing in ASEAN contributed to the effectiveness of the advertising. The apparent success of the BOI's campaign was not what could normally be expected from the use of image-building techniques. In only rare instances will a country benefit from such substantial and simultaneous interest on the part of such a large group of prospective foreign investors.

We were unable to uncover any evidence to demonstrate that other image-building activities, such as missions and seminars, have

Table 19. Japanese Capital Investment (Percentage of Total Foreign Capital Investment, 1985–87)

Country and item	1985	1986	1987
Thailand			
Applications	9.1	34.9	37.2
Approvals	9	53.4	43.1
Promotional certificates	20	10	70
Malaysia			
Applications	n.a.	15.6	24.8
Approvals	25.2	11.1	30.8
Indonesia			
New approvals	9	44	22.7
New & expansion approvals	14	40	36

n.a. Not available.

Note Percentages calculated from figures for the value of Japanese capital in investments applied for and approved and the value of total foreign capital in investments applied for and approved.

Source: Thailand-BOI; Malaysia-MIDA; Indonesia-BKPM.

been effective in building or changing images, since none of the promotion agencies we studied had conducted evaluations or contracted out evaluations of the effectiveness of these activities.

In sum, there is a substantial amount of evidence to suggest that advertising activities are not usually effective in generating investment directly. And there is no evidence in support of the effectiveness of other image-building activities in generating investment. There is some evidence, however, to suggest that advertising is effective in building and changing attitudes. This evidence requires acceptance of the view, accepted in most advertising circles, that recall of advertisements and advertising themes is indicative of changes in attitudes or is evidence of the creation of an image.

Effectiveness of Investment-Service Activities

Agencies do not regularly conduct systematic evaluations of their investment-service activities. In fact, we were able to uncover only one evaluation of investment-service activities. This one was conducted in association with the U.S. embassy in Kingston, Jamaica, and it did support the view that inefficient service to investors may reduce the extent of foreign direct investment.

In 1985 Jamaica's JNIP in association with the U.S. embassy in Kingston, carried out a survey of investors' attitudes to identify what current and prospective investors considered to be the incentives and disincentives to operating in Jamaica. The survey consisted of a series of interviews with companies in three categories: companies now operating in Jamaica, investors in the process of looking at Jamaica as a potential investment site, and companies operating in other Caribbean countries that decided not to invest in Jamaica. The interviewees were chosen from JNIP files. Industries targeted by the government of Jamaica for promotion, such as garment manufacturing, data entry, and electronics assembly, were emphasized in the selection of the interviewees.

The principal finding of the study was that "while the Prime Minister and the JNIP successfully promote Jamaica as an investment site, other government agencies integral to the investment process do not facilitate investment."[29] This conclusion was reached because one of the disincentives most frequently mentioned in the survey was bureaucracy in the investment approval process. In response to the findings from these interviews that the inadequacy of investment service was a serious disincentive to investment in Jamaica, the JNIP attempted to improve its investment service. The agency was influential in the establishment of a subcommittee of the cabinet, the Joint Investment Committee (JIC), to deal with problems that slowed the approval process for investors. The agency also simplified the process investors had to go through to apply for permits."[30]

Although we uncovered no systematic evaluations of investment-service activities, it was obvious that promotion agencies considered these activities effective in getting interested investors to make commitments to invest. Agencies other than the JNIP—Malaysia's MIDA and Thailand's BOI, for example—established within their agencies, centers or "one-stop shops," in which investors could make arrangements to obtain all the approvals and permits they needed to implement their investments. Further, in 1988 both Malaysia's MIDA and Costa Rica's CINDE established divisions devoted solely to the servicing of investors who had already begun operations in their respective countries. The actions of these agencies provide evidence of the importance with which they regard investment-service activities.

Effectiveness of Investment-Generating Activities

Many promotion agencies regularly evaluate their investment-generating activities. We supplemented these existing evaluations by interviewing responsible managers from U.S. corporations involved in thirty recent investment decisions. The investment decisions involved all ten investment localities represented by the investment promotion agencies in the study, with at least two investment decisions per locality. Because of the problems of access to data, the sample of investment decisions was not a random sample drawn from the population of such decisions for each country, but we are aware of no systematic biases that affect the results other than those that will be discussed later in this section. Information about these decisions and the decisionmakers responsible for them came from a variety of sources, including investment promotion agencies, U.S. chambers of commerce, U.S. embassies, press reports, central banks, consultants, and commercial banks in the countries that we studied.[31]

The managers were asked, among other things, about the influence of the promotion agency in their investment decision. They were asked to indicate whether investment promotion agencies had a significant influence, some influence, or no influence on the investment decision.[32] Regardless of the type of influence the manager suggested that the agency had on the decision, managers were asked how they came in contact with the promotion agency and who had initiated the contact. In addition, they were asked whether they had been exposed to any promotional techniques and if so what the effect of these techniques had been. The managers were also asked to evaluate the quality of service received by their firms throughout the decision period and after their firms had decided to invest. For an agency to be judged to have had a significant influence, the manager would have to indicate that the agency's influence was significant and also be able to identify a promotional technique used by the agency that made the agency's influence on the investment decision significant. Agencies would not have had to attract a company to a particular region, such as the EC, or the Caribbean Basin, but the agency would have had to be instrumental in attracting a company to a particular country within that region.

The criteria for agencies having had "some influence" were much less rigorous. The agency did not have to influence the company to consider the country but it did have to have been visible, available, and helpful, once an investment decision was contemplated, and to have provided an adequate service level in helping the company move toward implementation of a project. To have had "some influence" agencies would not have had to initiate contact with the company by way of some promotional technique, whereas this was necessary to a finding of "significant influence."

The sample of investment decisions was divided into investments oriented toward export markets and investments oriented toward the country's domestic market. This distinction was thought to be important because of the a priori hypothesis that investment promotion is more effective when aimed at investments oriented toward export rather than toward domestic markets. We felt that since investors considering projects for export could invest in many different countries, they would be more likely to be influenced by the promotional efforts of one country. Investors seeking to serve the local market of a particular country, however, could often do so only by investing in that country.

In eleven (37 percent) of the thirty investment decisions, the promotion agencies exerted a "significant influence," and in another nine decisions (30 percent) the agencies exerted "some influence." The degree of influence differed significantly, however, according to the market orientation of the project. In projects oriented toward the domestic market of host countries, there was not a single instance of "significant influence" and only one of "some influence." All eleven instances of "significant influence" were export-oriented investments, and in nineteen of the twenty-two export-oriented investments studied, promotion agencies exerted influence on the investment decision (see table 20).

The results of this research are consistent with what other researchers have discovered about the degree to which the investment decisions of companies can be influenced by the policies governments use to attract them. A recent study of investment incentives suggested that export-oriented investments are influenced by tax and similar incentives to a much greater degree than investments oriented toward a country's domestic market. The only policy variable that seems to have a significant influence on investments for the domestic market is protection.[33]

In response to questions about the promotional techniques that influenced their investment decisions, managers in the "significant influence" category indicated, in ten instances out of eleven that they had been personally approached by investment promoters who continued to work with their companies throughout the investment decision process. There was only one instance in which an investor was influenced by a promotional technique directed at a group of companies. This technique was a seminar targeted to selected companies in one industry—a specific investment seminar.

Table 20. The Influence of Promotion on Investment Decisions by Market Orientation of Investment Decision

Market orientation of project	Significant influence	Some influence	No influence	Total
	Level of influence			
Domestic	0	1	7	8
Export	11	8	3	22
Total	11	9	10	30

In fact, we were struck by the enthusiasm with which interviewees in the "significant influence" category regarded the efficacy of promotional activities that involved personal contact with the investor. The responses of three managers involved in export-oriented projects in three different countries is recorded below. The names of the companies and the promotion agencies have been omitted because assurances of confidentiality were given to all the managers that we interviewed:

> I had not had much experience with industrial development agencies prior to this investment decision, but I think that this agency has certainly done more to facilitate my company's entry into a country than any prior agency we had been involved with. I give the agency an A+ for persistence. Marketing representatives from the agency had been working with my company for over ten years prior to our eventual investment decision. These representatives would keep calling us and making presentations even when we were not considering an investment. When we did decide that it was time to invest in that area of the world, important personal contacts with the promotion agency had already been established. (A manufacturer of products for the analysis and purification of fluids.)
>
> Our final decision to invest in this country, instead of neighboring countries, was influenced very heavily by the legwork of the promotion agency. The agency's staff contacted us very early in the decision process, and they stayed with us throughout the decision time frame, doing an excellent job of packaging the country, of providing appropriate research information, and of getting our company access to all the facilities that we needed. The agency's marketers had already done research on our product line, so they could provide us with meaningful information about the investment possibilities, as opposed to the promotion officials of a neighboring country who focused on sending us general publications and who were not nearly as knowledgeable about issues of spe-

cific interest to our firm when we contacted them for information. (A manufacturer of electrical and security products.)

Our company made a strategic decision to commit to a region of the world, but then began a search for the "right" country to operate within. Our decision to invest in this country was influenced strongly by the professionalism, aggressiveness, and persistence of the investment promotion agency. My policy during the search process was to ignore agencies that sent me literature, unless this literature was followed up by telephone calls or a visit. Our firm was contacted repeatedly and often, but with much professionalism by the agency. The agency's representatives were effective, professional, smart, and aggressive. (A manufacturer of computer hardware and software.)

These responses from the managers we interviewed suggest that techniques involving direct contact with specific firms were effective in generating investment. This conclusion is consistent with at least one other independent evaluation of investment-generating activities. This evaluation was conducted by the Telesis Consultancy Group in 1981 as a part of a broader study of the effectiveness of IDA.[34] The research upon which this evaluation was based included interviews with IDA executives, managers from investing firms, and development agencies throughout Europe.

Attempts were made to calculate the market share of export-oriented investment achieved by various countries in Europe, and to calculate the cost-effectiveness of the grants and other incentives received by certain firms from IDA. In the context of investment promotion, the researchers found that:

both potential investors and other development agencies view the IDA as the premier organization in the field. The characteristics which have contributed to this success are well known in Ireland and have been perfected over many years of experience: *excellent market coverage through a large number of sales offices in different countries; a thorough and well targeted process of identifying prospects;* a command of media and promotional techniques; *aggressive and well planned sales procedures;* a one-stop-shop organization in Ireland; *effective capabilities for industrial intelligence, sectoral analysis, and financial analysis;* significant clout in "getting things done" for new prospects in Ireland; a well-developed and advanced factory program; the ability to provide quick responses to customer inquiries and to make quick decisions on approvals; and an intelligent and dedicated group of professionals working in an organization with a very impressive esprit de corps [emphasis added].[35]

Thus, evaluations conducted by investment promotion agencies themselves and independent evaluations suggest that direct contact with specific firms or an emphasis on personal selling is the most effective technique for generating investment directly.

The Effectiveness of Subcontracted Investment-Generating Activities. Many investment promotion agencies, however, have not relied upon promotional techniques that emphasize their own personal selling activities. Promotion agencies that subcontracted promotional activities were in this category. Most of the subcontracting that we observed was done by Thailand's BOI and Indonesia's BKPM.

Thailand. The BOI, as mentioned earlier, subcontracted investment-generating activities to Arthur D. Little, Inc. (ADL), financed by a $2.2 million grant from USAID covering the period 1983–86. The contract required ADL to be responsible for the following activities:

- Identify promising investment opportunities for promotion in the United States.
- Organize up to three investment promotion campaigns in the United States, targeted to an identified audience in specific industries.

- Develop a data base to support investment promotion activities during the term of the contract.
- Help the BOI assist interested U.S. investors through follow-up of promotion activities and by locating local Thai joint venture partners.
- Provide assistance to the BOI on BOI's investment promotion activities in the United States and in areas related to investment strategy and promotion.
- Develop and implement a monitoring program to evaluate the effectiveness of the effort under the contract.

USAID commissioned an economic consultant, Donald J. Rhatigan, to conduct an evaluation of the effectiveness of these promotional activities. The evaluation team interviewed representatives from USAID, the BOI, and groups in the private sector within Thailand, analyzed BOI investment statistics, and reviewed listings of investors and prospective investors that ADL had compiled under the evaluation section of the contract.[36] In the following paragraphs we have drawn heavily on this evaluation.

The principal component of the investment promotion program consisted of the three specific investment missions to the United States, in the electronics, metal fabricating, and agribusiness sectors. American firms were screened to identify those firms that had some interest in investing in Thailand. All firms were invited to general seminar presentations, but a smaller, high-priority group was invited to participate in one-on-one interviews with senior BOI officials and members of the Thai private sector. ADL estimated that a total of 500 companies, identified as potential investors, attended the general seminars, and BOI delegations met with 100 companies in the one-on-one sessions.

In the Rhatigan evaluation an attempt was made to identify results of the promotional activities in applications to the BOI for promotional privileges and actual start-up operations during the period of the contract. On the basis of an examination of BOI data and comparison with leads generated from the investment missions, it was found that these missions had resulted in one start-up, out of ten start-ups with American participation during the period of the promotional activities; five investment applications, out of a total of thirty-two applications from the United States during the same period; and an undetermined but modest number of sourcing arrangements. The contractors were found to have executed the terms of the contract in a technically competent manner, but it was also suggested that investment missions might not be the most effective promotional technique and that greater attention should be paid to other promotional techniques. The evaluation came to the following conclusion:

> If USAID is to continue to finance investment promotion activities, better research is required concerning methods of investment promotion, alternative to the large consulting organization, data bank based company search cum full blown (and expensive) public relations driven investment mission...
>
> An appropriate use of USAID resources would be to finance upgrading of the BOI's sector specific technical expertise. If USAID were to decide to continue to support BOI's promotional efforts in the U.S. market, financial and technical strengthening of the New York promotion office should receive higher priority than a repeat of the promotion campaigns.[37]

Indonesia. The BKPM also subcontracted investment-generating activities to private consulting firms. As in the case of the BOI, these activities were financed by USAID. The consulting firms, Business Advisory Indonesia (BAI) and Resources Management International (RMI), were responsible under the contract for preparing project profiles, providing consulting services to Indonesian and American investors, and—a responsibility added midway through the contract—conducting investment missions to the United States.

Project profiles were feasibility studies designed to provide estimates of the costs and potential profits associated with particular investment projects. Most promotion agencies that prepared these studies did so as part of their service function, in association with particular investors who already had an interest in investing in the country. The BKPM, however, prepared these profiles in advance, without the participation of particular investors. It saw these profiles as a tool that could attract investors.

In February 1986, USAID conducted the only evaluation of the performance of the consultant. It was a mid-term evaluation, since the contract would not expire until 1988, relying primarily on the tracking procedures of the consulting firms. Neither USAID nor the BKPM engaged in any independent research.

The evaluation suggested that neither USAID nor the consultants had been advocates of the use of project or industry profiles in investment promotion, but "USAID agreed to profiles in the scope of the work against our better judgment to keep BKPM happy."[38] The BKPM, it appeared, attempted to choose the projects that should be profiled on the basis of the government's priority list for investment (DSP), then matched project profiles with interested investors during the agency's investment missions abroad.[39] On the basis of information suggesting that profiles of projects such as glass fiber, single-cell protein, pumps and compressors, and pig farming had not generated any interest, despite the expense of preparing them, the USAID evaluation concluded that

> no more project profiles should be prepared—markets and conditions change too quickly to make the final product relevant, BKPM selection priorities do not reflect investor interest, our contractors do not have the in-house expertise to efficiently do the profiles, the potential investors have their own unique set of questions they need answered, and BKPM is not a promotion oriented agency willing to "market" a good profile if they ever really got one.[40]

In sum, the evaluation concluded, as had other promotion agencies, that the advanced preparation of project profiles was an ineffective tool for promoting foreign investment.

The consulting services to be provided under the contract, as discussed earlier, also required the consulting firms to provide the first twenty-five hours of consulting services to any American or Indonesian prospective investor at no cost to the client. These consulting hours could then be charged to USAID under the contract.

The evaluation concluded that the consulting activities resulted in several investments. The consulting firms received a total of 250 inquiries about free consulting services. They actually consulted with fifty-four American and Indonesian firms. Eight of these firms received the full twenty-five hours, and three, all U.S. firms, paid for additional time. The consultations resulted in six applications for investment, and of these applications, four investments seemed certain at the time of the evaluation. With these results, the mid-term evaluation recommended that the consulting portion of the contract be continued and expanded to offer fifty hours of free consulting to Indonesian firms.

USAID did not, however, ascertain whether the firms that were given the consulting services would have invested in Indonesia irrespective of the services of the consultants. One of the managers that we talked with during the course of this research indicated that the consulting services were very useful to his company in its analysis of the Indonesian marketplace but that these services did not attract the company to Indonesia. He indicated that the company would have gone ahead with its proposed investment even if the consulting services had not been available. A sample of one does not, of course, enable us to conclude that the consulting services did not lead to investments that would not otherwise have been made, but we do have our doubts. On the other hand, the provision of free consulting services may have provided an important incentive to the consulting firms themselves. Given the prospects of continuing work from investing firms, the consulting firms might have put a special effort into promotion.

After the mid-term evaluation, USAID and the BKPM requested that each of the consulting firms plan an investment mission to the United States. The BAI planned a mission to the West Coast of the

United States in February 1988, and RMI planned an investment mission to the East Coast in April 1988. In planning these investment missions, each consulting firm endeavored to target its mission to selected industries and to remedy the apparent deficiencies of earlier missions sponsored by the Indonesian government.

In planning its mission to the West Coast, BAI monitored carefully the number of government officials and Indonesian businessmen that would be invited to attend. The firm did not expect to have the usual complement of Indonesian businessmen, since it felt that American businessmen preferred to make a decision to invest in a particular country and then, if necessary, initiate a search for a joint venture partner, rather than have such a partner thrust upon the firm in the throes of its investment decision. Appropriate American companies were identified within particular sectors, such as specialty chemicals, rubber products, and food processing. BAI planned to arrange for Indonesian government representatives to visit ten of these companies, and then, after the mission, these companies would be followed up by the BAI's consulting associates on the West Coast. BAI expected that during the six months immediately following the mission, between three and five of the ten companies contacted would visit Indonesia. The achievement of this ratio of site visits to companies contacted would suggest that the mission was successful.

On the basis of BAI's internal evaluation, the mission was a success. Meetings were held with thirty-five U.S. companies, all of which were serious investment prospects. Most of the meetings were held at the headquarters of the mission, but representatives from Indonesia did visit three companies. The firm's consulting associates on the West Coast followed up leads obtained from the mission. By May 1988 the mission had resulted in two site visits to Indonesia by prospective investors. This did not meet the success criteria the firm had set for itself during the planning stage, but additional site visits by prospective investors were anticipated before the six-month period following the mission, which was to end in August 1988.

RMI, during the planning of its mission to the East Coast of the United States, also tried to take a different approach from the one typical of previous missions sponsored by the Indonesian government. In early 1988, the firm had identified twenty companies that had some interest in investing in Indonesia. RMI planned to use the mission to try to obtain from these firms commitments to invest in Indonesia.

Preliminary evaluations of the success of the RMI venture were mixed. RMI claimed that the mission was "a great success." More than 150 people attended one session, and approximately ninety private appointments between prospective Indonesian and U.S. joint venture partners were held during the course of the mission. Twelve letters of intent were signed by potential partners, and several other companies were said to be seriously pursuing opportunities discussed in the course of the sessions. An independent observer, however, concluded that, like previous missions sponsored by the Indonesian government, many of the U.S. businessmen in attendance at the mission already operated in Indonesia and, he was more skeptical about the ultimate effect the mission would have in generating new investment.

The evaluations of investment-generating activities made by contractors provide some mixed evidence about the effectiveness of the particular promotional techniques that were used by the contractors. There was little evidence that feasibility studies and consulting services attracted many investors, although they might possibly have been of assistance to an investor who was already interested. The independent evaluations of investment missions suggested that they were not consistently effective in generating investment, whereas evaluations performed by the firms involved in planning these missions suggested that they were effective in generating investment. Evaluations were more positive, perhaps, in those instances in which the structure of the arrangement gave the consultants a particularly strong incentive to perform well— that is, when attracting an investor would probably generate future consulting business for the contracting firm.

In sum, we suggest that the weight of the evidence supports the view that an appropriate mix of investment-generating activities can be quite effective in generating investment. The research findings indicate that investment leads may be uncovered by the less personal investment-generating activities such as direct mail campaigns and missions and seminars targeted to particular industries. Evidence to support the effectiveness of subcontracted investment-generating activities is quite shaky. The most effective investment-generating techniques, however, are clearly those that involve personal interaction and contact with decisionmakers in specific companies. This finding is consistent with the received wisdom on the most effective techniques for marketing industrial products. As one noted marketing analyst observes, "Although advertising, sales promotion, and publicity play an important role in the industrial promotional mix, personal selling serves as the main selling tool."[41] Thus, the less personal techniques, such as direct mail campaigns, telemarketing, missions, and seminars, even if targeted at specific industries, may be effective only if used as means to an end—identification of relevant decisionmakers in appropriate companies for direct contact—and not the primary tool to generate investment. There remains, however, the issue of whether these direct marketing, or other investment promotion activities are cost-effective.

Cost-Effectiveness of Investment Promotion Techniques

The task of measuring the cost-effectiveness of investment promotion is even more difficult, yet even more necessary, than that of measuring effectiveness. Based primarily upon the evaluations uncovered during the research, estimates of the cost and results of particular promotional techniques are recorded in table 21.

The data suggest quite different cost-effectiveness for different activities. Direct marketing activities resulted in promotional costs of $440 per job created. Consulting activities appear about equally cost-effective, at $436 per job. This result, however, has to be tem-

Table 21. The Costs and Results of Particular Promotional Activities

Promotional activity	Cost (thousands of U.S. dollars)	Results
Advertising[a]		
(IDA's 1986 program)	5,300	High measures of advertising recall (see tables 16, 17, 18)
Missions		
ADL mission (Thailand)[b]	500	1 investment, 5 applications
BAI mission (Indonesia)	100	2 site visits
RMI mission (Indonesia)	100	12 letters of intent
Trade shows (CINDE)	30	No investment interest
Direct marketing[c] (CINDE 1986)	2,200	5,000 jobs a year
Project Profiles (Indonesia) (eight completed by BAI/RMI)	220	No investment interest
Consulting (BAI/RMI) (Based on USAID evaluation)	240	4 investments, 550 jobs

a. The IDA program was used because no other agency provided information on the results of its advertising. The cost includes advertising, printing, and promotion expenses. See Industrial Development Authority of Ireland, *Annual Report* (Dublin, 1986), p. 71 for figures.

b. This information is derived from the Rhatigan evaluation of the ADL contract. On the basis of these figures, the evaluation posed significant reservations about the cost-effectiveness of missions as an investment promotion technique in Thailand and in other countries in which USAID had financed investment promotion activities.

c. Although many agencies conduct direct marketing activities, CINDE was used because the cost figures obtained from other agencies usually include the cost of promoting domestic investment. Further, the results obtained from other agencies invariably cover all investments entering the country, irrespective of the role of the promotion agency in attracting those investments. CINDE, on the other hand, did not promote domestic investment (before 1988), and did not maintain figures on all investments entering Costa Rica. The agency made a determined effort to count only those investments it attracted. CINDE's total operating cost was $2.5 million including $300,000 spent on advertising.

pered by the observation made earlier that the consulting activities may not have been responsible for attracting all the investment associated with them in the figures. Missions, trade shows, and project profiles were especially costly in relation to the investments that they generated. It is difficult to compare the cost of advertising with the cost of these other activities, since its focus is on changing attitudes rather than on directly generating investment.

The information recorded in table 21 on the costs of various promotional programs can be used to address two more questions about the cost-effectiveness of promotional activities. The first is: Do the costs of an efficient promotional program outweigh the benefits obtained from the investment attracted through such a program? We shall address this question through analyses, presented in tables 22 and 23, of the costs of promotion and the direct employment benefits of investment. We shall compare the costs with the benefits under a set of assumptions.

Table 22. The Costs of an Efficient Promotion Program

Assumptions
An average efficient program consists of:
  Image-building activities
  —$2 million campaign for one year[a]
  -$300,000 per year thereafter[b]
  Investment-generating activities—$440 per job[b]
Program attracts 5,000 jobs per year[b]
Government's discount rate 10 percent
Image-building campaign amortized over 9 years
Analysis

Annual amortized cost of image-building campaign ($2 million over 9 years at 10 percent)		
Cost per year	$347,000	
Annual actual cost of image-building activities	$300,000	
Total annual cost of image-building activities	$647,000	
Cost of image-building activities per job ($647,000/5,000 jobs)		$130
Cost of investment-generation activities per job ($2.2 million/5,000 jobs)		$440
Total cost per job (investment generation and image building)		$570

a. This estimate is for a relatively large-scale image-building program. It was derived, in part, from estimates of the cost of the image-building programs of Canada, Britain, and Ireland. Canada's 1985 program cost about $3 million; Britain's 1983 program cost about $1 million; and Ireland's 1986 program cost about $5 million. (The cost for Ireland includes the cost of printing and promotion expenses.)

b. These figures are all taken from the operations of CINDE in Costa Rica. CINDE's total budget of $2.5 million included about $300,000 for advertising and public relations. This agency attracted about 5,000 jobs per year. This leads to a cost for investment-generating activities of about $440 per job ($2.2 million/ 5,000 jobs).

Table 23. Cost of Promotion versus the Direct Employment Benefits of Investment

Assumptions
  $570 to attract one job via investment promotion[a]
  An investment life of 10 years
  A discount rate for the government of 10 percent
  Investment is export-oriented and all market prices = shadow prices
    except the price of labor
  Market price of labor = $.50 an hour[b]
  Shadow price of labor =70 percent of its market price
Analysis
  Cost of Promotion per job = $570
Direct Employment Benefits to Country
  Direct benefits per job per hour (market price – shadow price) = $.15
  Direct benefits per job per year $.15 x 40 hours x 52 weeks) = $312
  Benefits over life of investment ($312 discounted at 10 percent for 10
    years) = $1,917

a. This promotional cost was obtained from table 22.
b. This wage rate represents an average wage for low- to medium-wage countries.

In estimating the cost of an efficient investment promotion program in table 22, we assume, as suggested in chapter 2, that such a program comprises two sequential phases: a focus on image building and a focus on investment generation. We assume that image-building activities cost $2 million for an initial campaign. We also assume, on the basis of figures from Costa Rica's promotional program, that image-building activities cost $300,000 a year after the initial campaign, that investment-generating activities cost $440 per job, and that an average of 5,000 jobs are attracted each year. In addition, we assume that the government's discount rate is 10 percent and that the cost of a one-year image-building campaign can be amortized over the following nine years. These assumptions lead to an estimated cost of $570 per job attracted.

In comparing the cost of an efficient promotion program with the direct employment benefits generated by foreign investment other assumptions are necessary. We assume that all the prices paid by the investor for inputs reflect the value of these inputs to the economy except the price of labor, that there are no externalities, and that the exchange rate reflects the shadow price of foreign exchange. We assume in the base case that the shadow price of labor is 70 percent of its market price. Thus, 30 percent of the wage bill represents benefits to the economy not captured in the firm's accounts. For the base case, we also assume a project life of 10 years, a discount rate of 10 percent for the government, and a market price of $.50 an hour for labor.

The results of calculations for the base case (see table 23) suggest that efficient investment promotion activities are highly cost-effective. The analysis indicates that promotional expenditure of $570 incurred to attract one job can bring benefits with a present value of $1,917 to the country. In table 24 we shall examine the sensitivity of this conclusion to changes in various assumptions.

Table 24. Sensitivity Analysis on Costs of Promotion versus Direct Employment Benefits of Investment

Cost of promotion: $570

Base case assumptions:	Market price of labor = $.50 an hour
	Shadow price of labor = 70 percent
	Investment life =10 years
	Government discount rate = 10 percent
	Direct employment benefits = $1,917
Alternate case 1:	Market price of labor = $.20 to $1 an hour
	Other assumptions same as base case
	Direct employment benefits = $767 to $3,834
Alternate case 2:	Shadow price of labor = 90 percent to 50 percent
	Other assumptions same as base case
	Direct employment benefits = $639 to $3,195
Alternate case 3:	Investment life = 5 years to 15 years
	Other assumptions same as base case
	Direct employment benefits =$1,183 to $2,373
Alternate case 4:	Government discount rate =15 percent to 5 percent.
	Other assumptions same as base case
	Direct employment benefits = $1,566 to $2,409

This analysis suggests that the conclusions from the base case results are not strongly affected by changes in the assumptions. The most sensitive assumptions are those about the cost of labor and its shadow price. In situations in which labor rates are lower than $0.20 an hour or the shadow wage rate is greater than 90 percent, even an efficient investment promotion program is not likely to be cost-effective.

There are, however, few countries in which labor rates are as low as $0.20 an hour. Those countries in which shadow wage rates are as high as 90 percent are probably near full employment. For these countries, investment is only beneficial to the extent that it provides advantages to the country other than increases in employment. Although our calculations were focused on employment because that was the benefit most valued by the authorities we interviewed, in other countries other benefits might dominate. In these instances similar calculations, using appropriate shadow prices, can be used to examine the cost-effectiveness of an investment promotion program.

There remains one additional question related to the cost-effectiveness of investment promotion: Are there techniques cheaper than investment promotion that a government can use to attract investment? We have indicated throughout this study that promotion is only one marketing technique a government can use to attract investment. Earlier research has suggested that governments can attract investment through pricing policies such as investment incentives, for example. The most popular incentive used by governments in developing countries is the tax holiday. In table 25, we shall examine and compare the cost of promotion with the cost of tax holidays to see the relative cost-effectiveness of these two techniques.

For this calculation, some additional assumptions are required. We assume that each job was associated with $20,000 of investment (a rough average for the projects in the study). Further, we assume that an investor's taxable profits would be 15 percent of the investment, and that the host country's tax rate is 40 percent. The calculations in table 25 were made for a $1 million project.

Table 25. The Cost of Promotion versus the Cost of Tax Holidays

Assumptions
  $570 to attract one job via investment promotion (see table 22)
  $1 million of investment
  A capital/labor ratio of $20,000 per worker[a]
  A rate of return on investment of 15 percent
  A tax rate of 40 percent

Analysis
  Cost of promotion
    Number of people employed = 50($1,000,000/ $20,000)
    Cost of promoting jobs = *$28,500* (50@ $570)
  Cost of tax holidays
    Annual profits = $150,000 ($1,000,000 @15 percent)
    Taxes forgone =$60,000 ($150,000 @40 percent)
  Cost of promotion in terms of tax holidays
    $28,500/$60,000 = *5.7 months of tax holidays*

a. The research uncovered widely varying capital/labor ratios, with ranges of $10,000 to $60,000 per worker. An average ratio of $20,000 per worker was used.

The analysis suggests that the promotion costs incurred in attracting investment are equivalent to granting 5.7 months of tax holidays to the investor. Most countries offer tax holidays of from five to ten years to attract investment. No official would, we think, believe that six months of tax holidays would attract a project. In situations where the techniques of promotion and tax holidays are completely substitutable and equally effective in attracting investment, investment promotion seems to be the more cost-effective technique. This conclusion is even more significant because in the calculation of the cost of tax holidays it was assumed that all holidays would be given to investors who would not otherwise have invested. Tax incentives, however, are generally awarded according to fairly inflexible rules. Thus, many firms might receive these incentives even though they would have invested without them. For the calculations of the cost of promotion, however, figures from an agency that makes a determined effort to count only those projects attracted by its promotional efforts were used.

In table 26, we shall examine the conclusion that promotion is less costly than tax holidays further by analyzing how sensitive the results recorded in table 25 are to changes in the base assumptions.

The results of the sensitivity analysis show that the conclusion that an efficient investment promotion program is likely to be more cost-effective than a program of tax holidays is not sensitive to significant changes in any of the basic assumptions of the relative cost analysis.

We conclude that an efficient investment promotion program is likely to be worth conducting for many countries. If the market wage rate is significantly greater than the shadow wage rate, as is often the case, employment benefits outweigh the costs of attracting the investment. Research done by others suggests that techniques other than promotion can also attract investment.[42] We

Table 26. Sensitivity Analysis of Costs of Promotion versus Costs of Tax Holidays

Cost of promotion: $570	
Base case assumptions:	$1 million of investment
	A capital/labor ratio of $20,000 per worker
	A rate of return on investment of 15 percent
	A tax rate of 40 percent
	Cost of promotion in tax holidays = 5.7 months
Alternative case 1:	Capital labor ratio =10,000 to 60,000
	Other assumptions same as base case
	Cost of promotion in tax holidays (months) =11 to 2
Alternate case 2:	Rate of return on investment = 5 percent to 25 percent
	Other assumptions same as base case
	Cost of promotion in tax holidays (months) =17 to 3
Alternate case 3:	Tax rate =10 percent to 50 percent
	Other assumptions same as base case
	Cost of promotion in tax holidays (months) = 23 to 5

conclude from our research, however, that investment promotion attracts investment at lower cost than at least one alternative technique, tax holidays.

Effectiveness of Government versus Quasi-Government Organization

Governments must choose not only the techniques that they will use in their promotional activities, on the basis of indicators of effectiveness and cost-effectiveness, but also the promotional structures that they will adopt. During the research we uncovered no evaluations of the relative effectiveness of different promotional structures. Given the lack of data on this important subject, and in an attempt to obtain preliminary results on the effectiveness of different structures, we separated the data we obtained on the influence agencies had on particular investment decisions into two groups on the basis of the two most popular structures identified in this research, government and quasi-government agencies.

The initial analysis was made of all the investment decisions, both export-oriented and domestic-oriented. Table 27 shows that of the eleven investments in which promotion agencies had a significant influence, only one investment was influenced significantly by a government agency, while the other ten were influenced significantly by quasi-government agencies.

This analysis was repeated using only export-oriented investments. The second analysis was performed because export-oriented investments had been identified as those most likely to be influ-

Table 27. The Influence of Promotion on Investment Decisions by Structure of Promotion Agency

Structure of promotion agency	Level of influence			
	Significant influence	Some influence	No influence	Total
Government agencies	1	2	8	11
Quasi-government agencies	10	7	2	19
Total investment decisions	11	9	10	30

enced by promotion agencies, and there was a greater proportion of domestic-oriented investment in the sample of government agencies than in the sample of quasi-government agencies. There were twenty-two export-oriented decisions. Government agencies were relevant in six of these. In one, their influence was significant; in another two they had some influence. In contrast, quasi-government agencies exerted a significant influence in ten out of sixteen investment decisions (see table 28).

We suggest that several factors, discussed in greater detail earlier, account for the apparent finding that quasi-government agencies have been more successful at promoting investment than government agencies.

In government agencies the investment promotion function is often a subsidiary function of the organization. The primary function is usually screening foreign investment and negotiating with foreign investors. Consistent with the conclusions of other researchers, we found that organizations established with the primary purpose of screening investment find it more difficult to promote investment than organizations, such as the quasi-government organizations, that are set up as marketing organizations.[43]

Further, since government organizations do not have reputations as marketing organizations and often find themselves constrained by the civil service salary structure, they find it difficult to attract the marketing skills required for successful investment promotion. As a consequence, they tend to rely on diplomatic staff to

Table 28. The Influence of Promotion on Export-Oriented Investment Decisions by Structure of Promotion Agency

Structure of promotion agency	Level of influence			
	Significant influence	Some influence	No influence	Total
Government agencies	1	2	3	6
Quasi-government agencies	10	6	0	16
Total export-oriented investment decisions	11	8	3	22

conduct overseas marketing. Diplomatic staff are usually not trained or experienced in marketing. Further, they often give the investment promotion function little attention, because it is usually a part-time activity and because they are usually not subjected to a control system that motivates them to perform adequately or penalizes them for performing inadequately.

Most government organizations have attempted to correct the problem of their inadequate supply of marketing skills by subcontracting investment promotion activities to the private sector or by seconding employees from the private sector. In some instances these contractors have perhaps performed well; in others they have certainly performed poorly. At least one evaluation of the performance of subcontractors suggests that they do not give sufficient thought to the design of promotional activities and as a consequence do not use the most appropriate promotional techniques.[44] We uncovered no evaluations of the seconding of employees from the private sector, another way such organizations attempt to overcome the shortage of marketing skills. It does not seem, however, that government agencies have completely overcome the problems that they often face as they attempt to promote investment through the use of either of these techniques. It is for these reasons that we conclude that government agencies have not been as effective as quasi-government agencies in promoting investment.

In sum, the evidence examined in this chapter shows that agencies adopt different processes to evaluate the promotional techniques that they use. Agencies that conduct investment-generating activities in-house integrate the evaluation process for these activities into their management control systems. The evaluations of other activities in which these agencies engage, and evaluations of the promotional techniques used by other agencies, are not integrated in this manner.

The agencies that evaluate investment-generating activities frequently and systematically have observed that the techniques most effective in generating investment are those that involve personal and direct relations with prospective investors. Independent evaluations of investment promotion activities and research in the related area of industrial marketing support this conclusion. These techniques are also cost-effective; they can generate employment benefits that exceed their costs, and they are less costly than at least one alternative technique used to attract investment, the tax holiday.

Finally, there is some evidence to suggest that quasi-government agencies, with their ability to handle well both the public and the private tasks that comprise investment promotion, have been more effective at the investment promotion function.

Notes

1. Where evaluations of investment-seevice activities take place on a regular basis, they might provide one indicator that agendas are demend-oriented—that is, willing to concentrate on identifying and responding to the needs of potential investors. A demand orientation was considered an important ingredient of successful investment promotion by researchers who studied the promotional efforts of American states. See John K Ryans. Jr.. and William I. Shanklin, *Guide to Marketing for Economic Development* (Columbus, Ohio: Publishing Horizons, 1986) p. 94.

2. Jamuna P. Agarwal, "Determinants of Foreign Direct Investment: A Survey," *Weltwirtschaftliches Archiv* 116 (1980): 739.

3. This information was obtained from International Monetary Fund, *Balance of Payments Statistics* (Washington, D.C., 1986/1987); 1985 data were used in the analysis.

4. See, for example. Friedrich Schneider and Bruno S. Frey, "Economic and Political Determinants of Foreign Direct Investment," *World Development* 13 (no. 2, 1985): 161–75; and John H. Dunning, "Explaining the International Direct Investment Position of Countries: Towards a Dynamic or Developmental Approach," *Weltwirtschaftliches Archiv* 117 (no. 1,1981): 30–64.

5. The most comprehensive study in this genre, in which the significance of forty-four economic, social, political, and policy variables was tested, was conducted by Root and Ahmed; see Franklin R. Root and Ahmed A. Ahmed, "The Influence of Policy Instruments on Manufacturing Direct Foreign Investment in Developing Countries," *Journal of International Business Studies,* Winter 1978, 81–93; and Franklin R. Root and Ahmed A. Ahmed, "Empirical Determinants of Manufacturing Direct Foreign Investment in Developing Countries," *Economic Development and Cultural Change* 27 (July 1979): 751–67.

6. See Dunning, "Explaining the International Direct Investment Position of Countries"; and John H. Dunning, "The Determinants of International Production," *Oxford Economic Papers* 25 (November 1973).

7. We used 1984 per capita CNP data so that this variable would lag the dependent variable by one year. The data were based on World Dank figures. See World Bank, *World Development Report* (New York: Oxford University Press, 1986, 1987).

8. The growth variable was measured by the growth of GNP per capita in 1984, on the basis of World Bank figures. See World Bank, *World Development Report.*

9. See Schneider and Frey, "Economic and Political Determinants of Foreign Direct Investment."

10. See, for example, Dunning, 'The Determinants of International Production," for the influence of the balance of payments; and Mario Levis, "Does Political Instability in Developing Countries Affect Foreign Investment Flows? An Empirical Examination," *Management International Review* 19 (1979): 59–68, for the influence of the balance of payments and inflation.

11. Inflation figures were obtained from World Bank data, and balance of payments information was obtained from IMF data, for 1984. See World Bank, *World Development Report,* and International Monetary Fund, *Balance of Payments Statistics.* In the model, following Schneider and Frey, a

balance of payments deficit was measured positively and a balance of payments surplus was measured negatively, leading to an expected negative relation between the investment and current account variables.

12. See Raghbir S. Basi, *Determinants of United States Private Direct Investments in Foreign Countries* (Kent, Ohio: Kent State University Press, 1963); and Yair Aharoni, *The Foreign Investment Decision Process* (Boston: Division of Research, Harvard Business School, 1963).

13. See Root and Ahmed, "Empirical Determinants of Manufacturing Direct Investment."

14. See Levis, "Doss Political Instability in Developing Countries Affect Foreign Investment Flows?"

15. See Frost & Sullivan, Inc., "The 1964 Political Climate for International Business: A Forecast of Risk in 80 Countries," The PolitIcal Risk Services Division (New York: Frost & Sullivan, December 1983). Countries were ranked according to the likelihood of political turmoil, defined to include activities such as labor strife, terrorist activity, public demonstrations, guerilla warfare, and international war. Countries with the highest turmoil rankings were given the lowest scores.

16. Investment promotion was measured using a dichotomous variable. The criterion was simply whether or not countries had a promotional presence in the United States during the period 1960–85. Countries that had such a presence were given the dummy variable -1; countries that did not have a presence were given the dummy variable -0. The use of a five-year period was chosen because discussions with managers from investing firms and government promotion officials suggested that the gestation period for an investment could be as long as five years. The use of a promotional presence in the United States as the benchmark to determine whether countries were actively promoting investment is not ideal, but in the absence of more comprehensive data on world-wide promotion efforts, it was considered a reasonable proxy. Our primary research on three continents suggested that countries that decided to promote foreign investment actively would invariably consider the United States a prime source

of capital and seek to establish a presence in that country. Data on the existence of a promotional presence in the United States came from "World Wide Guide to Foreign Investment," *Business Facilities Magazine* (New Jersey), various issues.

17. See Root and Ahmed, "Influence of Policy Instruments on Manufacturing Direct Foreign Investment in Developing Countries," for a study that includes the following six policy variables: corporate taxation, the complexity or simplicity of tax incentive laws, the country's attitude toward joint ventures, the extent of local content requirements, and limitations on foreign personnel. Of these only the corporate taxation variable was statistically significant.

18. Multiplediscriminant analysis was used by Root and Ahmed in-stead of multiple regression analysis because the researchers used categorical rather than continuous variables to measure investment flows. Similarly, Dunning used multiple discriminant analysis in the construction of clusters that were then analyzed using multiple regression techniques. See Root and Ahmed, "Empirical Determinants of Manufacturing Foreign Direct Investment in Developing Countries," and John Dunning, "Explaining the International Direct Investment Position of Countries." For one of the studies using multiple regression analysis, see Schneider and Frey, "Economic and Political Determinants of Foreign Direct Investment." The authors express dissatisfaction with the methodologies employed by some other researchers, indicating that some studies are unnecessarily complicated and difficult to interpret and that others are close to "measurement without theory," the researchers apparently having engaged in ad hoc searches for variables that may have a significant influence. Levis used stepwise multiple regression as a mechanism to select variables; see Levis, "Does Political Instability in Developing Countries Affect Foreign Investment Flows."

19. Although the distribution of a natural variable might be skewed, the distribution of the logarithm of that variable is often nearly symmetric and sometimes nearly normal. See Robert Schlaifer and Arthur Schleifer, Jr., *Analysis of Quantitative Data* (Boston: Harvard Business School, 1981), p. 40.

20. The individual contributions to R^2 were calculated by taking the squares of the conditionally standardized coefficients.

21. See, for example, Levis, "Does Political Instability in Developing Countries Affect Foreign Investment Flows?"

22. This finding agrees with the research of Reuber, who found that the flow of FDI per capita into developing countries was correlated with their GDP but not with the growth of their GDP. See Grant L Reuber, *Private Foreign Investment in Development* (Oxford: Clarendon Press, 1973).

23. These tests included examination of the Hatmax, Sizcor, and Durbin Watson statistics statistics and a Krasker-Welsch test for bounded influence in the Analysis of Quantitative Data (AQD) regression package and the use of principal components to attempt to detect the existence of multicollinearity.

24. Researchers have suggested, however, that tax incentives may not be effective in attracting foreign investment. See, for example, Louis T. Wells, "Investment Incentives: An Unnecessary Debate," *The CTC Reporter* 22 (Autumn 1986): 58–60 and Reuber, *PrivateForeign Investment in Development.*

25. See US. Embassy (Kingston) and the Jamaica National Investment Promotion Ltd. *Incentives and Disincentives to Investment in Jamaica.* Kingston, Jamaica, August 19, 1985, p. 2.

26. Studies of advertising in a corporate setting have emphasized the importance of establishing advertising objectives, conducting benchmark surveys, and conducting postcampaign surveys to ascertain the effectiveness of particular advertising campaigns. For an early but seminal article on this subject. see Russell H. Colley. "Squeezing the Waste Out of Advertising," *Harvard Business Review,* September–October 1962. pp. 76–88.

27. See, David Ogilvy and Joel Raphaelson, "Research on Advertising Techniques that Work—and Don't Work," *Harvard Business Review.* July–August 1982, pp. 14–22.

28. See "BOI re-thinking Japanese investment amid influx," *Bangkok Post*, January 27, 1988.

29. See "Incentives and Disincentives to Investment in Jamaica."

30. The JNIP was not empowered to grant approvals to investors, but it tried to make this task easier for the investor by appointing an economic development executive (EDE) to each investor and by giving the EDE the job of obtaining all the approvals an investor needed. Before this change, the investor had to fill out up to forty-seven forms seeking approvals of one kind or another. After the change, the EDE would fill out only one form from data obtained from the investor. See Jamaica National Investment Promotion. *Business Jamaica,* January–February 1967, p.3.

31. The distribution of managers surveyed, by country, was as follows: for six countries there were two investment decisions per country, for one country there were three investment decisions, and for three countries there were five investment decisions per country. The position of the managers interviewed varied with the company. In all instances the manager was integrally involved in the investment decision. For some cotantries this responsible manager was the general manager, managing director,.or CEO; in others it was a vice-president of marketing or international, a plant manager, a director of special products, or a manager of new markets. Some interviews were conducted in person, others were telephone interviews. In all interviews a common guideline was used that elicited information about the importance of investment promotion in the investment decision, both in attracting the firm to the country and in follow-up activities, including the service of the promotion agency. We also obtained information about whether the project was for export or domestic markets, the nature of the project, and the principal activities of the firm undertaking the project.

32. This methodology follows that used by Basi in a survey study to identify the possible determinants of foreign direct investment. Basi uses the categorization crucially important, fairly important, or not important. See Basi, *Determinants of Unitrf States Private Direct Invest ments in Foreign Countries,* p.10.

33. For a description of the research project, see S. Guisinger and Associates, *Investment Incentives and Performance Requirements* (New York: Praeger, 1985). For an analysis of the research findings as they are related to export-oriented versus domestic-oriented investment, see Wells, "Investment Incentives."

34. ThIs report, although critical of the level of grants offered by the IDA, concluding that the grants, although cost-effective, were higher than they needed to be given Ireland's share of the market for internationally mobile investment in Western Europe, and of IDA's policymaking function, contending that the organization was too powerful, found IDA's personal selling and direct marketing approach to investment promotion effective. See Telesis Consultancy Group, *A Review of Industrial Policy in Ireland* (Dublin: National Economic and Social Council, 1982).

35. See Telesis Consultancy Group, *A Review,* p. 172.

36. See Donald J. Rhatigan and Associates, *Final Evaluation of Private Sector in Development* (Washington, D.C.: TVT Associates, July 1987).

37. See Rhatigan, *Final Evaluation,* pp. 25, 27.

38. See Memorandum on "Private Sector Development Project-Evaluation of BKPM Investment Promotion Contracts," February 19, 1986.

39. The priority list for investment (DSP) is the Indonesian government's listing of the fields of investment that are open to foreign and domestic private investment. The list consists of four categories: fields of investment that are open to foreign investment; fields that are open to domestic investment; fields that are open to small-scale enterprises; and fields that are closed to all types of further investment. For the 1987 list, see Republic of Indonesia, *Priority List for Investment,* 1987 (Jakarta, May 1987).

40. See. "Memorandum on Private Sector Development Project," p. 4.

41. Quoted from Philip Kotler. *Marketing Management: Analysis, Planning, and Control* (Englewood Cliffs, New Jersey: Prentice Hall, 1984) p. 164. See also Urban B. Ozanne and Gilbert Churchill, Jr., "Adoption Research: Information Sources in the Industrial Purchase Decision," *Proceedings,* Fall Conference (Chicago: American Marketing Association, 1968) for a statement that during the interest and evaluation stages of an industrial buying decision (corresponding to the in-vestment-generating stage of investment promotion) personal selling and the provision of technical sources of information are the most important selling techniques.

42. See Guisinger, *Investment Incentives.*

43. See for example, Dennis J. Encarnation and Louis T. Wells, Jr., Sovereignty en Garde: Negotiating with Foreign Investors," *International Organization* 39 (Winter 1985): 71.

44. See Donald Rhatigan, *Final Evaluation,* pp. 24–27.

5

Conclusion

An important conclusion of this research is that an efficient investment promotion program can attract certain types of investors to a country at a cost that is significantly less than the value of the direct benefits the country receives from the investment. Further, the research reveals a great deal about what makes up an effective investment promotion program. Investment promotion is not, however, the only marketing technique that a government can use to attract investors. A government, in its attempts to attract investors, is faced with the challenge of designing an appropriate marketing mix for investment. Although the principal focus of this study is on promotion, the information we obtained about the costs of various promotion programs and the circumstances under which promotion seems to be most effective allows us to draw tentative conclusions about the role of product and price in the investment marketing mix and the relative cost-effectiveness of the marketing techniques of promotion and price.

The Effectiveness of Investment Promotion

On the basis of the findings of this research, we came to several conclusions about the effectiveness of investment promotion.

Promotion and Export-Oriented Investment. An investment promotion program appears to be most successful in attracting investors to a country if it is focused on export-oriented investment, whether for export to world markets or to regional markets. We uncovered no evidence to suggest that investment promotion activities were effective in attracting firms to a country to serve the domestic market. For such firms, it would appear, the domestic market itself is the attraction; to reach that market, investment elsewhere is unlikely to be a feasible alternative. Firms that are seeking sites to serve export markets, however, can choose from a wide range of countries. For these firms, this research suggests that investment promotion—and prior research suggests that pricing via incentives—is likely to have an impact on their investment decisions.[1]

For most governments trying to attract domestic-oriented investment, the primary concern should be the product—that is, the country's investment climate and the inherent attractiveness of its domestic market. To attract investors who plan to serve the domestic market there appears to be less need to allocate resources to investment promotion and, according to other research, to investment incentives. For export-oriented investment on the other hand, while an attractive product remains essential, promotion and pricing, if well managed, can be significant factors in attracting investors.[2]

This is an argument on the other side: According to one school of thought, investment promotion should also be effective in attracting domestic-oriented investment because promotion is capable of reducing the information costs associated with investing in certain locations, especially countries, such as China, with complex investment climates. We uncovered no evidence to support this position. On the other hand, we do not think our data are sufficiently comprehensive to refute it for all cases.

The marketing techniques of promotion, pricing, and product need to be employed in a complementary manner during an investment promotion program geared to attracting investment. We would expect, however, that a country's success in attracting investment will lead to improvements in the country's investment climate; this improvement will substitute for the effects of promotion and pricing. Thus, in situations in which countries have continued success in generating investment, a decline might be expected in the need for resources to be devoted to promotion and to the provision of incentives.[3]

The Costs and Benefits of Investment Promotion. The benefits a country gains from an efficient promotion program geared to attracting export-oriented investment usually exceed the costs of attracting the investment. In this research we compared the costs of an efficient investment promotion program to the direct employment benefits obtained from investment attracted by the program. From this analysis, we conclude that the direct employment benefits produced by foreign investment exceed the typical costs of attracting this investment, except where a country has very low wage rates, or where a country is very near full employment. Countries in which wages are very low, if they promote at all, should have closely targeted promotion programs that cost less per job created than a typical promotion program. Countries that are near full employment should be promoting investment only to obtain benefits other than employment, of course.

The Relative Costs of Promotion and Incentives. Since there are other marketing techniques a government can use to attract investment, such as pricing by way of investment incentives, the question remained whether there are techniques that can attract investment more cheaply than investment promotion. After comparing the costs of an efficient investment promotion program with the costs to the government of one type of investment incentive, the tax holiday, we found that an efficient investment promotion program is less costly than a typical program of tax holidays. This is not to say that tax incentives have no function, but for most countries, resources devoted to promotion have a chance at generating much better returns than would those same resources devoted to longer tax holidays.

We therefore suggest that an efficient investment promotion program is both effective and cost-effective. On the basis of our findings in this research, in the remainder of this chapter we shall recommend ways of making an investment promotion program efficient. In designing such a program, governments can benefit if investment promotion is regarded as a type of industrial marketing. Further, they should recognize that the organization that is to handle investment promotion needs to be able to conduct a range of tasks, including some that are more typical of private organizations and others that are usually associated with government organizations.

Investment Promotion as a Type of Industrial Marketing

It may be productive to regard investment promotion as a type of industrial marketing, with which it has close parallels. In both investment promotion and industrial marketing, similar organizations are making large, relatively infrequent, well-researched, "purchase" decisions: In this study we propose that since the investment decision is similar to the industrial buying decision, the research on the way corporations make industrial purchases and on the way other companies market industrial products is germane to an understanding of the mix of marketing and promotional techniques that is most effective in attracting firms to invest in a country.

Information Sources in the Investment Decision

The empirical findings of this study suggest that, similar to the industrial buying decision, promotion is a significant factor in the investment decision only in instances in which governments use appropriate promotional techniques to attract investors in different stages of the investment decision process. Research in industrial marketing suggests that in making the decision to purchase a new product, a buying unit within a corporation or an institution goes through several stages, beginning with initial awareness of the product and ending with the final purchase.

At each stage of this decision process different promotional media are more effective. During the initial stage the more effective promotional techniques are impersonal ones such as advertising. In the final stages, the more effective techniques involve personal contacts from the seller's representatives or from other firms that can provide testimonials. We discovered that the same relationship holds in investment promotion. Impersonal techniques, such as advertising, seem to be more effective in influencing investors who are in the early stages of the investment decision process, while personal techniques, such as presentations tailored to specific companies, are the only techniques that seem to be effective in influencing investors who are in the later stages of the process.

Investment Promotion Strategies

Indeed, the promotion agencies we studied tended to adapt to the decision processes of their target markets by using primarily impersonal promotional techniques to build awareness or images in the investment community before attempting to generate investment more directly. Many agencies moved to a focus on investment generation once appropriate images had been formed and used more personal techniques thereafter to generate investment directly. In many instances agencies changed focus as they adapted to the decision processes of their target market. We suggest that in most instances this promotional strategy is an appropriate way to manage the investment promotion function.

We do, however, suggest that there may be instances in which the usual sequence that we observed may be inappropriate. If a country already has a favorable image among investors, there should be no need to devote significant resources to image building. Further, if a country has a particularly bad reputation for the intractability of its bureaucracy for example, and that reputation indeed reflects the facts, then investment promotion efforts might begin with service activities. It may be essential to make existing investors happy and to ease the way for new investors before initiating any effort at image building. Indeed, if the country has any particularly unattractive features for foreign investors—in addition to a difficult bureaucracy political instability or an extremely overvalued exchange rate, for example—an image-building campaign started before the "product" is set right is, at best, likely to be a waste of resources. Only when the country can offer itself as an attractive site for at least certain kinds of investment should it engage in an image-building program.[4] Decisionmakers in firms with the capacity to invest abroad are, after all, a sophisticated group of "consumers." These persons, before committing the capital of their firm, are likely to scan the environment for information about the investment climate of a particular country. It is unlikely that they will rely solely on the information they obtain from the host government's promotional organization. Promotion agencies should try to work with their governments to design policies to improve the investment climates of their countries. The agencies can then attempt to build images that take into account these changes in government policy.[5]

Image-Building. An investment promotion agency just beginning an investment promotion program should do so by first deciding the range of firms that it might reasonably hope to attract to its country. Industrial countries need not focus on particular industries. The less developed the country, however, the more important it is for that country to begin promotional efforts by targeting particular sectors, industries, or firms. These countries are likely to be considered seriously by only a few groups of potential investors. Accordingly, it would not be cost-effective for them to mount general image-building programs.

After an agency, in collaboration with the appropriate government department or departments, has decided what group of investors it will seek to attract, it should find out what image these investors have of the country. If investors have a favorable image the agency can begin active efforts to court them.

Investors may, however, have an unfavorable image of the country even though such an image does not reflect the facts. Usually such images are simply out of date.[6] In such instances, promotion agencies should attempt to correct the unfavorable images before attempting to generate investment. These image-building activities are an important prerequisite to attempts to generate investment directly, because, like the buyer of an industrial product, a potential investor must have some interest in an investment site long before a decision is made to invest.

Evaluating Image-Building Activities. Agencies should have a clear program to ascertain the effectiveness of their image-building activities in building or changing images by evaluating particular advertising campaigns, missions, and seminars. In evaluating the activities, they should make two distinct measurements: they should measure the perceptions or attitudes of the population that has been targeted before the start of these activities, and they should measure the perceptions or attitudes of this population after the image-building activities. Without these measurements it is virtually impossible to evaluate the effectiveness of particular techniques.

The techniques of measurement need not be complicated. Investors can be surveyed to determine their attitudes toward investing in a particular country. If an advertising campaign then seems warranted, investors could be surveyed again, after the campaign, to ascertain whether their attitudes have changed. Participants in seminars can even be asked to complete carefully worded questionnaires before and after the seminar to elicit information about the usefulness of the seminar in creating an awareness of, or correcting perceptions about, the country's investment climate.

Investment Generation. Promotion agencies should begin active efforts to generate investment when their evaluations suggest that at least certain groups of targeted investors have favorable images of the country and are willing to consider it as a possible investment site. An agency might decide to target additional investors, however, or there could be significant changes in a country's investment climate that would make the prevailing images of investors obsolete. If such changes occur, the agency should engage in image-building activities even while it attempts to generate investment directly, or in extreme situations it might best go back to a focus on building images.

In order to generate investment effectively, agencies should use promotional techniques that involve personal, direct contact with investors, instead of impersonal techniques that try to attract groups of investors simultaneously. This approach to investment promotion dictates that an agency should establish an overseas marketing presence that would allow its investment promoters to be physically close to prospective investors.

Such a presence does not have to comprise a large network of well-staffed overseas offices. As in all facets of investment promotion there are cost-benefit trade-offs. The size and scope of an overseas promotional presence should be related to a variety of factors, including the size of the country and its level of development. Small, developing countries may need to establish only a few, or possibly even one, overseas office.[7] Of course, for larger countries and for more highly developed countries, an effective investment-generating program requires the commitment of significant resources to the maintenance of an overseas promotional presence.

Evaluating Investment-Generating Activities. These research findings suggest that investment-generating activities are most successful when they involve direct approach with specific companies and when the promoters who contact the companies are good marketers who engage in promotional activities on a full-time basis. In addition, this strategy requires the agency to implement an appropriate program of evaluation, which should be based on the presumption that the activities of an individual investment promoter can be tied directly to an investment. If evaluation is based on this presumption, an agency can measure the extent to which each promoter is successful in attracting investment. These measures then provide a basis for rewarding successful promoters.

We found that evaluation programs such as the one described above appeared with greater frequency in some types of promotional organization than in others.

The Public-Private Choice in Investment Promotion

In examining the way governments choose a structure in which to conduct investment promotion activities we found that most of the organizational issues fell within the realm of the public-private choice of management of certain nontraditional government activities.

Appropriate Organization for Investment Promotion

Like some other activities financed by governments, investment promotion has certain characteristics of tasks typically carried out by the government but others that are normally associated with tasks usually located in the private sector. Activities of this type are often financed by a government because they generate social profits that are greater than the private profits they could provide. When this condition prevails, a government must either finance the activity or risk that it will be underprovided.

Governments can adopt two polar positions in their attempts to carry out the nontraditional government activity of investment promotion. A government can carry out investment promotion itself, but this approach has the disadvantage that the government organization may be unable to acquire skills that are required if the activity is to be managed properly. The required skills may reside in the private sector and be difficult to attract to the public sector, especially with the salary constraints typical of civil services. Accordingly, if the government decides to manage the activity, it may also, through various methods, have to take steps to obtain the appropriate skills from the private sector.

An alternative approach is for the government to delegate the management of investment promotion activities to the private sec-

tor. This approach often has the disadvantage that the private sector will not handle well the attributes of the task that are more like
traditional government tasks, such as servicing investors by acquiring permits and approvals from other government departments.
Indeed, neither the wholly public nor the wholly private approach
to the management of investment promotion is ideal. Regardless
of the approach that is chosen there will be management issues
with respect to the way the inherent disadvantages of either approach are to be overcome. In an attempt to overcome these disadvantages, governments may search for the organizational
approaches that combine most effectively the skills and resources
of both the public and the private sectors.

Indeed, we observed that many governments did avoid these
two extreme approaches and, instead, chose an intermediate approach. They conducted investment promotion through quasi-
government organizations. These organizations, while reporting
to the government, were not enmeshed within the conventional
government and civil-service structure. Separation from the conventional apparatus of government gave these organizations certain inherent advantages over government organizations in carrying
out the investment promotion function. At the same time these
quasi-government organizations had an advantage over private
organizations in conducting the tasks of investment promotion
that required close contact with the government since they were,
in fact, part of the government.

In contrast to government organizations, quasi-government
organizations tended to be created for the purpose of marketing
countries as investment sites and not with the primary objectives
of screening investment or negotiating with investors. These agencies had the flexibility to attract personnel with the marketing expertise successful investment promotion requires. In addition, they
were able to obtain sufficient autonomy to design and implement
promotion strategies, and to develop integrated management control systems that tied the activities of marketers to particular investments. These management control systems provided sufficient,

timely information with which agencies could simultaneously control, evaluate, and motivate marketing representatives. The overseas offices of quasi-government agencies also tended to be staffed by full-time promoters who were directly controlled by, and accountable to, the agencies. These advantages were particularly important when an agency was heavily involved in investment-generating activities.

In contrast to private organizations, however, the quasi-government agencies did not face the problems likely to be faced by a private agency in conducting the investment promotion tasks that are more like typical government tasks, such as servicing investors and cooperating with the government.

These research findings build a strong case for the location of a government's promotion program in a quasi-government organization. Many countries, however, already have promotional programs. If such a program resides in a conventional government organization or in a private organization, change may be difficult. For government organizations, conversion to quasi-government status may be politically unacceptable. Nevertheless, certain management practices may lead to better performance in both government and private organizations.

Management Practices to Improve Organizational Effectiveness

Like several of the quasi-government agencies that we studied, government agencies should design comprehensive management control systems so as to tie the activities of marketing representatives to particular investments. Further, since the effectiveness of these organizations is often reduced because they coexist with the countries' screening functions, the promotion program should be separated to the greatest extent possible from the screening function. After all, screening and promotion activities require completely different skills and approaches. At a minimum, the promotional program should reside in a separate division of the organization. The promotion organization often desires to capture the screening organization, seeing some of its investors turned away. And the screening organization often wishes to capture the promotion organization, if for no other reason than to capture its large budget. Both desires should be resisted; these are two separate functions.

In fact, government agencies usually have few of the skills that investment promotion requires. They are often forced to rely on diplomatic staff, who are not trained or experienced in marketing.[8] We suggest that government organizations can make the promotional efforts of diplomats more effective by establishing control systems that monitor the performance of diplomatic staff. This monitoring function is made easier if the agency can arrange to use diplomatic staff on a full-time basis instead of part-time. Even if this reduces the overall scope of the organization's overseas promotional presence, empirical observations suggest that it makes this presence more effective.

Increasing the Effectiveness of Contracted Activities. Government agencies have tried to overcome the problem of their lack of marketing skills by contracting promotional activities to the private sector, instead of conducting these activities in-house. This research suggests that investment-generating activities are, in the long run, probably done better in-house than by contractors. Outside contractors are generally not very good at following up investment leads through periods that may at times be long. Financial and personnel constraints in many countries, however, may require that contracts be made with outside organizations.

Agencies that do contract out investment-generating activities should ensure that they participate in the design of the promotion program. These programs should not rely on impersonal activities, such as missions and seminars, but should emphasize the identification of firms that are investment prospects and the development of ongoing personal relationships with these firms. Agencies should also conduct independent evaluations of these contracts and not rely solely on the tracking procedures of the contractors. One suggestion for improving the effectiveness with which the contractors perform these promotional activities is to include bonus clauses in the contracts that would allow the contractor to increase earnings by generating additional investment. Such a clause would indicate that both the agency and the contractor adhere to the philosophy that a particular contractor, like an individual overseas marketer, can make a difference in attracting investment. The Indonesian experience with consulting firms suggests that agencies can provide an incentive for performance on the part of contractors by making investors into potential clients of the contractor.

Management Practices in Private Agencies. A private agency needs to develop cooperative working relations with the government. The government should probably be involved in developing strategic plans for the organization, including decisions about the types of firm to which promotional efforts will be directed. Service to investors is one of the more difficult tasks faced by private promotion organizations. To improve performance of this task, promoters within these agencies should be evaluated on the basis of their ability to serve investors and not only on their ability to attract them.

Maximizing the Effects of Foreign Assistance. Finally, regardless of the type of organization involved, whether government, quasi-government, or private, we observed that agencies in the developing countries that we studied were often engaged in the search for external resources to complement what their governments were willing to spend on investment promotion. More significant, multilateral agencies, development assistance organizations from some industrial countries, and foreign firms were often willing to assist agencies from these countries with financial and other resources. We suggest that agencies from developing countries make determined efforts to take advantage of these resources. Since of this group foreign firms are least likely to offer their assistance, the agencies from developing countries should take the initiative in finding out whether these firms will be willing to assist them in their investment promotion efforts.

In order for development assistance organizations, such as USAID, to maximize the effectiveness of the promotion programs in the developing countries in which they have provided resources, we recommend that each organization assist in designing promotion programs based on its positive and negative experiences with investment promotion in other countries in which it has been involved. This requires an exchange of information among aid missions. We observed that this straightforward management practice was not always followed.

Not all countries face identical problems in attracting foreign investors. The sample of countries that we studied did not include all possibilities. Little-known countries, with small and scattered populations, for example, may find image building particularly difficult and expensive. Similarly, countries with recent records of extreme hostility toward foreign investment may find changing perceptions to be a more difficult task than did the countries we studied. Nevertheless, we believe that the lessons we have been able to draw from the countries that we studied have wide applicability. Further, and perhaps more important, we believe that the kind of analysis that helped us to understand the promotion problems of these few countries can be applied to the design of appropriate investment promotion programs for a wide range of other countries, even though the programs themselves may differ considerably from those that we observed.

Notes

1. See, for example, Louis T. Wells, Jr., "Investment Incentives: An Unnecessary Debate," *The CTC Reporter* no.22 (Autumn 1986): 58–60; and Stephen E. Guisinger and Associates, *Investment Incentives and Performance Requirements* (New York: Praeger, 1985).

2. The stark difference between the greater need for promotion and pricing in the attempt to attract export-oriented investment rather than domestic-oriented investment explains the difference between the use of

promotion and pricing by individual U.S. states and by the U.S. federal government. The individual states emphasize promotion and pricing, since they are primarily seeking investment that will serve a broader market than their particular state (export-oriented). Foreign investors usually have the entire U.S. market in mind when contemplating an investment in a particular state. From the point of view of the federal government, however, most foreign investment is domestic-oriented, since the principal attraction is the U.S. market. Accordingly, there has been no pressure for federal authorities to begin a national program of investment promotion. For information on the extensive programs of promotion and incentives employed by various states, see John K. Ryans, Jr., and William I. Shanklin, *Guide to Marketing for Economic Development* (Columbus, Ohio: Publishing Horizons. 1986) p. 94.; and Dennis J. Encarnation. "Cross-Investment: A Second Front of Economic Rivalry." in *America versus Japan: A Comparative Study,* ed. Thomas K. McCraw (Boston: Harvard Business School Press, 1986).

3. There is some evidence that both Ireland's IDA and Singapore's EDB reduced the scope of their promotion programs slightly between the mid-1960s and 1988. During this period, Ireland's IDA reduced the incentives that it gave to investors, although there was little reduction in the scope of its promotional presence. The strategy of reducing expenditure on incentives before reducing expenditure on promotion is consistent with the findings of this research, which, on the basis of estimates of the costs of promotion versus the costs of incentives such as tax holidays, are that promotion is probably more cost-effective than tax holidays. In the case of Singapore, the EDB reduced its promotional presence slightly during the 1980s and, also during this period, reduced the incentives it was willing to offer investors, although the country had always tried to offer incentives on a targeted basis. In 1988 more than 50 percent of the country's foreign investment came in the form of reinvestment from existing firms. Further, Singapore was importing labor on a daily basis from Malaysia to cope with a severe labor shortage. Given these conditions of full employment and an increasing proportion of investment coming in the form of reinvestment, further reductions in the EDB's overseas investment promotion program and in its incentive program seemed imminent.

4. The results of recent research on the way corporations build images suggest that corporations that do not have high-quality marketing reputations should seek to develop that reputation among a narrowly selected group of customers before trying to generate high visibility for the company. Many developing countries have poor reputations as investment locations. It is important for these countries to develop credibility among a carefully chosen group of investors before engaging in high-visibility image-building efforts. See, for example, Thomas J. Kosnik, "Corporate Positioning: How to Assess and Build a Company's Reputation," working paper (Boston: Harvard Business School). In Kosnik's image-building matrix, the preferred route for a company to take in building an image is to move from "Unknown" (low visibility and low credibility) to "Undiscovered" (low visibility and high credibility) and eventually to "Unparalleled" (high visibility and high credibility). Broad attempts to build an image before a company has generated credibility in any market segment could lead to an "Undesirable" status (high visibility and low credibility). When a company has an 'Undesirable" Status, negative news about its marketing program is widely circulated. It becomes very difficult for such a company to reach an "Unparalleled" status. We suggest that a country seeking foreign investment faces a similar set of issues.

5. During the research we uncovered several examples of this sequence of marketing activities. Most image-building campaigns began after changes in government policy that, in essence, represented product or price changes. During the early 1970s, for example, Malaysia's FIDA proposed that the government adopt a specific incentive structure before making its promotional efforts that were focused on U.S. semiconductor firms. The incentive legislation that was adopted stipulated that all companies entering Malaysia within a two-year period would be granted pioneer status, making them eligible for ten-year tax holidays. Companies that did not invest in Malaysia during this two-year period would be ineligible for these tax incentives.

6. Investors could have misperceptions about particular aspects of an investment climate because they were never aware of the true nature of a climate that had always been favorable or because recent changes in an investment climate made the existing perceptions of investors obsolete.

The instance of Investment Canada fits the latter category. This agency needed only to use the marketing technique of promotion when Canadian government policy changed the country's restrictive investment climate to one more favorable to investment. In-vestment incentives were not necessary because of the inherent attractiveness of the country as a location for investment, once government roadblocks to investment had been removed.

7. In 1987, for example, the small Caribbean nation of St. Lucia (238 square miles, population 140,000) had one overseas investment promotion office, which was located in New York. This office was staffed by one professional who conducted personal promotional activities by relying heavily on direct mail and telemarketing and the intensive follow-up of leads generated from these techniques. Since the promotional program began, St. Lucia has moved from 43rd to 27th in international ranking as a location for U.S. electronics firms; moved to 6th place in the entire Western Hemisphere, behind Canada, Mexico, Costa Rica, Barbados, and Jamaica; and to third place in the Caribbean, behind Barbados and Jamaica, as a relocation and expansion site for U.S. electronics firms. The director of the promotion agency maintained that St. Lucia's rise in prominence as a relocation site for U.S. electronics manufacturers is "a direct result of the country's increased promotional activities." The rankings of countries, based on a survey of 760 firms by the Electronics Location File, were listed in a variety of publications, including *Caribbean Business.* May 9, 1984; *Silicon Valley Technical News*, May 21, 1984; and *Business Facilities*, May 1984.

8. The observation that diplomatic staff are not good at marketing and promotion activities has been noted in earlier evaluations of in-vestment promotion activities. See International Policy Analysis, As *Analysis of Investment Promotion Activities* (Washington: SRI International, 1984) pp. 53–54; and Ludwig Rudel, "The Feasibility of Establishing a Service in the U.S. to Facilitate Business Linkages between U.S. and LDC firms," Asia and Near East Bureau, U.S. Agency for International Development, March 1, 1986, p.6.

Afterword

Revisiting *Marketing a Country: Promotion as a Tool for Attracting Foreign Investment*

Louis T. Wells
Harvard Graduate School of Business Administration

It has been 10 years since Alvin Wint and I finished the research for the monograph entitled *Marketing a Country: Promotion as a Tool for Attracting Foreign Investment*.[1] The intervening decade has seen the formation of new investment- promotion agencies, more money spent on trying to attract foreign investment, and numerous experiments in how to go about the task. Despite the widespread efforts of developing countries to attract investors, foreign investment remains strikingly concentrated in only a small number of countries. Thus, data support what we all know from casual observation: that not every promotion effort has succeeded. This paper reports some of what I and others have learned from the accomplishments and failures of various promotion agencies over the past 10 years.

Basic Activities of Promotion Agencies

The original monograph of *Marketing a Country* described three basic investment-promotion techniques: image building, investment generation, and investor services. It argued that the mix of these techniques provides a good indicator of the strategy of a promotion agency. It further posited that the weight assigned to these techniques, or the strategy of an agency, should reflect the task that the particular country faces in marketing itself to investors. For example, a country that has recently changed its policies toward foreign direct investment could benefit from an emphasis on image building, since it might need to convey new information to potential investors who would otherwise be unaware of the changes. In contrast, a country with a long-established favorable investment climate ought to consider emphasizing the more difficult investment-generation techniques.

Policy Reform as a Basic Promotion Function

The classification of techniques proposed in *Marketing a Country* has become the standard terminology for describing the main activities of investment-promotion agencies. If the paper were to be written today, however, a fourth technique, policy advocacy, would be added to the three described in the monograph. Advocating improvements in the foreign investment climate has become an extremely important activity of several promotion agencies. And it is fairly certain that the failure of a number of those agencies to improve the climate has been one reason for the failure of many countries to attract the anticipated volume of foreign investment. Consider two examples of agencies that have emphasized the improvement of the investment climate:

In Mozambique, the national investment-promotion agency (CPI) has become deeply involved in trying to reduce the bureaucratic red tape that investors face. The history of socialism in Mozambique has led to a sharp disconnect between new investment policies announced by top government officials and the implementation of those policies throughout the bureaucracy. Thus, as policies have changed, reform of the bureaucracy has become critical, since it has served as a barrier to investment. CPI's major role in improving the investment climate began after it participated in a series of private sector conferences in which discussion of bureaucratic barriers was high on the agenda.

Colombia's investment-promotion agency (COINVERTIR) has, for reasons different from those driving Mozambique's agency, begun to devote a major part of its activities to policy and bureaucratic reform. In both countries reform efforts are linked to the provision of services to investors. Providing service to investors—during negotiation and implementation in Mozambique, or in the operating stage in Colombia—gives promotion agencies detailed knowledge about the problems investors face. It is knowledge of this kind of detail that enables the agencies to be effective champions of reform. Top officials in governmental ministries do not usually know exactly what hurdles confront investors; as a result, they find it difficult to take the necessary steps to ensure that new policies are implemented effectively.

For example, when foreign investors in Colombia complained about the documentation required of them before they could remit dividends abroad, high-level Colombian officials answered that the elimination of exchange controls should have eliminated the documentation problems. But COINVERTIR collected specific information on the required documentation that remained even after foreign exchange policies had been liberalized. Top managers at the central bank were unaware that cumbersome procedures survived after the need for them had disappeared. This detailed information allowed COINVERTIR to press for change.

In Mozambique, CPI undertook a serious effort to assist an investor who was building a large aluminum smelter.[2] The project had the backing of high-level officials who supported a rather formal structure that developed during the negotiation stage and was retained, in a modified form, to help the investor overcome bureaucratic problems encountered during implementation of the project. Assistance in the negotiation and implementation stages enabled CPI officials to learn about problems with company registration, customs clearance, temporary registration of automobiles, obtaining tax rulings, and a host of other details. In reform-minded Mozambique, this kind of information made it possible for CPI to play a special and useful role with individual ministries and agencies, as well as with an interministerial committee dedicated to reducing bureaucratic barriers. CPI negotiated with bureaucrats to solve problems for the investor constructing the aluminum smelter; those solutions can now be applied to assist future investors. Moreover, through working closely with the one investor, CPI's staff developed the contacts in other agencies that will enable it to guide future investors through the labyrinth of controls that remained. At the same time, CPI began to build support for eliminating some of the tedious procedures required of investors.

In other cases, barriers to foreign investment result not so much from bureaucratic procedure, but from broader policies. When, for instance, many investors identified weak infrastructure in Costa Rica as a major disadvantage in attracting the kinds of investment the country wanted, Costa Rica's investment-promotion agency (CINDE), supported policies to reform the state-owned telecommunications and power companies. CINDE organized conferences in the country and abroad to seek support for solutions to the problem.

In Mozambique and Colombia, championing reform played a major role in the promotion process for special reasons. In Colombia domestic unrest meant that image-building or investment-generation activities abroad would not have been effective and may have been counterproductive. As long as the country was in turmoil, the promotion agency found it useful to focus on serving investors already in the country, hoping to retain and encourage them to expand their projects. The knowledge gleaned from serving existing investors led COINVERTIR officials to identify areas where reform had been frustrated by the bureaucracy. In advocating reform, COINVERTIR hoped it could establish support for reinvestment, and, with eventual domestic stabilization, could foster a better climate that would stimulate new investment in the future. In Mozambique, the red tape remaining from the old bureaucratic mindset meant that the country was probably not ready for a major image-building effort abroad. In addition, the Mozambican promotion agency simply could not command the resources for an image-building program. In both countries, promotion agencies played a very productive role in assisting incoming investors in the implementation stage or existing investors during their operations, which led to a very productive role for promotion agencies in advocating improvements in the investment climate and thereby encouraged future investment inflows.

Types of Services to Investors

Marketing a Country described two types of investor services. Although the monograph did not explicitly use the terms, today these two services have come to be known as pre-investment-decision and post-investment-decision services. If I were writing the paper today, I would break the services into three categories: pre-investment-decision, implementation, and post-investment services. The distinctions are useful because the three kinds of services play very different roles in investment promotion. The mix of these services delivered by an agency ought to be considered carefully, and the choices should be tied to the overall strategy of the agency.

Services in the pre-investment-decision stage are provided very well by a number of agencies; hardly at all, by others. This category of services includes giving potential investors information about the country and about procedures required of investors. Some investment-promotion agencies provide only very general information, often only macroeconomic data. In contrast, other agencies provide detailed data, sometimes customized to the needs of particular kinds of investors. Thus, CINDE, in Costa Rica, gives prospective investors not only wage rates but also rates that are paid by specific kinds of firms. CINDE can provide a detailed schedule of power costs, by volume and by location. In this pre-investment category, a number of agencies also provide services that facilitate prospective investors' visits to the countries. CINDE, for example, will meet potential investors at the airport, accompany them through immigration and customs, provide a car and driver, and set up appointments for visits with other investors. These appointments also typically include Costa Rican government officials, suppliers of infrastructure and other services, and members of scientific institutions, embassies, industry chambers, and universities. Although this kind of service is not especially expensive to provide, it does require a great deal of organization. As a result, some agencies that try to provide it are not very effective in doing so.

Services in the implementation stage help investors through the process of building their projects. In some countries, this kind of service is provided perfectly well by private sector groups. Often, a few law or accounting firms specialize in assisting the investor. But where these services are not well organized or prove too expensive, investment-promotion agencies have on occasion assumed this function. Other reasons for the close involvement of investment-promotion agencies in these services include helping agencies to understand the problems that investors face. The resulting knowledge has greatly benefited agencies in their role as advocates of policy and procedure reform. The experience described earlier of CPI in Mozambique illustrates the gains that accrue to agencies from involving themselves in the implementation stage.

Services provided in the post-investment stage are based on the belief that satisfied investors ultimately expand their operations and help to attract other investors to a country. Post-investment services comprise efforts to assist companies to overcome problems they encounter while they are operating. These kinds of services also help the promotion agency to identify barriers to further investment, as the Colombian experience suggests. In fact, in countries unable to attract many new investors, perhaps because of domestic unrest, post-investment activities and associated efforts to improve the investment climate are occasionally the principal activities of investment-promotion agencies and often become closely linked to policy advocacy.

Management Issues

Marketing a Country included a chapter on how investment-promotion agencies are structured in various countries. That chapter focused on the relationship between the agency and the government. It described relationships in which agencies were a part of the traditional civil service, private agencies completely divorced from government, and agencies that could be labeled as "quasi-government," that is, they belonged to and were financed by the government, but they were not subject to the usual constraints of the civil service and other bureaucratic rules. The monograph then listed advantages and disadvantages of each approach. Those arguments for and against each approach still apply today. Some of the management problems of promotion agencies, however, did not receive as much attention in the monograph as they would if the paper were written today.

Fundamental Problems

The core management problems facing promotion agencies today derive from three characteristics of investment promotion: it is a public good, it requires skills that bridge the public and private sectors, and performance is difficult to measure.

The original monograph pointed out that investment promotion is a public good. The benefits of bringing foreign investors to a country are captured broadly, not by a specific organization that can collect part of the benefits as fees to pay for its services.[3]

Marketing a Country also suggested the difficulties in staffing a promotion agency with people that have appropriate skills. The agency must successfully interact with government to be of service to investors when they are implementing their projects and to influence policy and the bureaucracy. On the other hand, it must have people who are oriented toward sales. These kinds of marketing people are rare in the public sector, and they earn high salaries in the private sector. It is especially important for an agency director to be able to bridge the public and private sector. Assembling these skills can prove to be a daunting management task.

Measuring the performance of an agency, or its employees, is difficult for three reasons: it is not easy to attribute investment to a particular cause, the results from investment promotion may come long after the activities that originally influenced the investment, and many of the barriers to foreign investment lie outside the control of the agency.

Financing Promotion Activities

The public-good aspect of investment promotion suggests that promotion should be a government-funded activity. Government funding, however, does not necessarily imply that the organization performing the activity has to be government owned. Often, government contracts with private parties to provide services for which government pays. In many countries, roads, for example, may be constructed by private contractors, although the costs of construction are paid by the government. On the other hand, when a public good is provided and the performance of the organization providing the service is especially difficult to measure precisely, government ownership usually follows. Since investment promotion is not only a public good, but the contribution of the agency is also hard to evaluate, especially on a short-term basis, public finance and public ownership almost invariably result.

Nevertheless, the original monograph cited one example of a private investment-promotion agency—CINDE. Finding a private agency was something of a surprise, given the arguments for government ownership. It would be more helpful now to describe CINDE as a nongovernment agency, or at least a non-Costa Rican-government agency, rather than calling it private. As *Marketing a Country* pointed out, CINDE was created with U.S. Agency for International Development (USAID) funding—hardly a private source. Moreover, as the decline of the Sandanista regime in Nicaragua led USAID to scale back its contributions in Costa Rica, CINDE continued to depend for most of its financing on a foundation created from assets recovered from other USAID programs and on income from CINDE's own assets that it had "saved" during the period of USAID financing. This "private" investment-promotion agency was not a profit-making institution. It did not charge for its services, and it received no funding from the private sector. It was, more accurately, a nonprofit organization that was the product of a government that was not Costa Rican. As such, it is not an example easily copied elsewhere.

In spite of CINDE's strong performance, some of the most important lessons to be learned from its experience are negative ones. CINDE continued to experience the problem that *Marketing a Country* described or predicted for nongovernment entities: weak relations with the government. Until 1999, tensions over the role of the agency in representing the country and in advocating policy change had not been adequately resolved. Government officials remained suspicious and jealous, suspecting that CINDE was spending more than it claimed and that its professionals were extraordinarily well paid, in comparison to most government employees. Further, CINDE had, on occasion, been accused of building private domestic and foreign support for particular policy changes. CINDE had not taken substantial steps to improve its relationship with the government. It had, for example, no government representatives on its board, and it operated in a rather opaque way, encouraging speculation about its operations.

In 1999, CINDE's future was in question. Funding from the foundation created from USAID-generated assets could soon disappear. But it was uncertain whether the government was willing to fund an organization that it found controversial. The uncertainty had already caused job turnover among CINDE's professionals. It seemed that the loss of good people would cause a deterioration in the performance of the organization. The career risk was real; the behavior of employees, thus, understandable. In fact, elsewhere (the Dominican Republic, for example) agencies supported with aid money had declined in size and quality, or had disappeared entirely as foreign aid funding was phased out.

If aid agencies or multilaterals are to finance the activities of investment-promotion agencies, they must plan at the outset for the day when their funding ends. Good planning is likely to lead to a long transition period in which government and the external providers of finance share the cost burden. (Receiving a substantial endowment from the foreign aid agency is, of course, a possibility for continuance.) The need to obtain eventual government support may mean that the agency has to be more integrated into government from the outset than was CINDE; otherwise, government is unlikely to assume funding as foreign sources dry up. In 1999, the World Bank and bilateral aid financed investment promotion in several countries. In some of those cases, the investment-promotion agencies appeared to be better integrated into government than CINDE, even though the agencies still managed to avoid some of the restrictions of civil service rules (in Mozambique, for example, where World Bank funding accounted for a part of CPI's budget). Better integration may increase the odds that the government will eventually provide funding.

Although *Marketing a Country* did not report on any such agencies, a few investment-promotion organizations have attempted partial or even total self-funding. One approach has been to charge for services. The results have not been encouraging.

A promotion agency must fund some mix of image building, investment-generation activities, and investor services. In most cases, only the last of these activities creates private benefits. Not surprisingly, this last function is also the one for which the private sector has, in many countries, stepped in to provide services, accounting for the spread of law, accounting, and other consulting firms that promise to help investors examine the country, prepare feasibility studies, and navigate the bureaucracy. When investment agencies have tried to provide these services and charge fees for them, they have found themselves in head-to-head competition with the private sector and thus unable to collect sufficient fees to pay for the service and for the other activities that are more public good in nature. At the same time, by charging and by competing with the private sector, these agencies have risked undermining their credibility as representatives of government. Some of these efforts, and their failures, are described in the Foreign Investment Advisory Service (FIAS) paper, "Strengthening Investment Promotion Agencies: The Role of the Private Sector."[4]

Some agencies have tried an alternative way of raising funds themselves: they have asked corporations for donations, usually in the form of "membership" fees. To a varying extent, they have claimed that incoming foreign investment generates externalities that benefit local firms and other foreign firms already in the country. Thus, new foreign investors provide customers for the goods and services of local firms. And more foreign investors provide more influence for existing foreign investors. In both Venezuela and Colombia, the corporate sector was asked to contribute substantial sums to the promotion agencies. Unfortunately, the results have also not been encouraging. Despite some enthusiasm in the first year or two, most contributing firms soon lost interest. Correspondingly, donations dropped off.[5]

Foreigners as Promoters

Investment-promotion agencies are subject to budgets, of course; but the problems mentioned above tend to place especially tight constraints on their expenditures. Not surprisingly, they constantly seek ways to leverage their existing resources. Some efforts have proved successful, while some have worked only under very special conditions. And some, it seems, have consistently failed.

Marketing a Country reported the efforts of the Thailand Board of Investment (BOI) to enlist existing foreign investors as "mini ambassadors." As such, they were to assist the BOI in its investment-promotion efforts. The monograph did not, however, uncover another phenomenon that has, sometimes unwittingly, enlisted other foreigners as effective promoters. Foreign managers of export processing zones and industrial estates have proved, on occasion, to be excellent investment promoters. The reason for their success is that they provide an important exception to the rule that promotion benefits cannot be captured by a private organization.

In a number of cases, even where official national promotion efforts have been minimal, managers of industrial estates and export processing zones have undertaken effective campaigns to attract investors. Two industrial estates outside Jakarta, Indonesia, for example, are managed by major Japanese firms. These managers have very successfully recruited Japanese manufacturers to produce in the zones. Similarly, the first viable export processing zone in Vietnam, with investors, was a Taiwan-operated zone near Ho Chi Minh City. The early investors were, of course, from Taiwan.

Managers of estates and export processing zones have a strong incentive to find investors, if their returns are based on rents and fees from the firms that manufacture in the zone. And zone managers from home countries of investors often have contacts with potential investors and can easily reach them to present the advantages their sites offer. In some cases, investors feel more comfortable with zones run by their own nationals. This appears to be especially true of the Japanese managers of two industrial estates owned by the Japanese near Jakarta.[6]

Foreign management of zones and estates does periodically result from the investment-promotion efforts of agencies in neighboring countries (discussed later in this paper). It is usual for this kind of management to have established industrial or export zones abroad for some kind of self interest. That interest can be met only by attracting firms into the zone. Thus, the affiliate of the Singapore investment promotion agency (EDB) that ran a zone on Batam Island, Indonesia, actively sought to bring investors in Singapore to the Indonesian zone. Similarly, in 1999 Mozambique, recognizing the promotional possibilities, showed an interest in working with Mauritius for a zone in Mozambique.

Subcontracting

Actual subcontracting of promotional activities is sometimes considered to be another way of leveraging resources. *Marketing a Country* took a rather strong position against subcontracting. Indeed, when the study was carried out, subcontracting had proved almost universally unproductive. The difficulty of measuring the performance of a subcontractor was almost certainly a major factor in explaining the failures of efforts to have consulting firms, for example, perform part of the promotional activities.

However, it now appears that there are certain cases where subcontracting can be effective. These situations occur when the kind of investor being sought can be narrowly defined, there are few candidate enterprises, and the nature of the project is very clear. When these conditions are met, the skills required are specific and performance can usually be measured. In fact, the criteria are usually satisfied when foreign investors are wanted for the privatization of state-owned enterprises. For example, when a foreign investor is needed to acquire a telephone company, there are only a few potential buyers in the world. It is necessary to have an entity that is trusted by the potential investors and that will bring the acquisition to investors' attention. In several countries, this task has been performed well by investment banking firms. If properly chosen, they know the industry well, possess the required trustworthiness, and have access to investors.

In fact, in the special case of privatization, it is probably better that the investment agency *not* become the principal promoter. Privatizations are usually one-time deals. It makes little sense for an agency with scarce resources to try to develop the contacts and expertise for one or two transactions. It is better to hire the skills from outside, usually from investment bankers, even though they charge high prices for their services. Given the nonrepetitive nature of the transactions, paying for outside services is likely to be cheaper than developing in-house skills that will not be used regularly in the future.

Merging Investment Promotion with Other Activities

In another kind of effort to leverage resources, many countries have been tempted to charge their embassies abroad with carrying out investment promotion. On the surface, this option appears attractive, since embassies already have a presence in the home countries of investors. The marginal costs of having officers in those embassies perform investment promotion appear to be low. But *Marketing a Country* explains the reasons why folding investment promotion into a country's embassies abroad has, in almost all cases, failed. Officials in embassies are trained in skills different from those required for promotion. They do not have the business background required to be effective in investment promotion. Moreover, their careers are advanced by successfully accomplishing tasks that are very different from investment promotion.

That is not to say that there is no role for embassies in investment promotion. Indeed, they should be provided with literature on investment in the country, since potential investors will on occasion contact them. And, they should be encouraged to forward information about any requests they receive to the investment-promotion office for follow-up. But they almost never provide good investment-promotion activities themselves.

Although *Marketing a Country* did cover the temptation to use embassies for promotion, it did not explore another commonly proposed method of conserving resources: combining investment promotion with export promotion. Proposals for this combination also have an easy appeal: if offices related to promotion have to be established abroad, why not combine investment and export promotion in order to save money? Again, these efforts have usually failed, because these two promotion activities are far more different than they first appear.

The differences between investment promotion and export promotion can perhaps be best understood by an analogy: the differences between marketing major industrial plant to companies and selling supplies or finished goods to firms or retail customers. For a company, the purchase of a major plant is an expensive and infrequent decision. It usually has strategic implications. The decision is therefore usually taken at a very high level in the enterprise. Many data are considered, and discussion occurs over a long period of time. In contrast, purchases of finished goods or supplies are usually frequent and routine. Supplies must meet specified standards, but as long as the standards are met and the source can deliver on schedule, the sourcing decision usually does not have strategic implications for the purchasing enterprise. Such decisions are generally delegated to a lower level of management, and they are often made quickly.

Reaching and convincing top management to locate in a particular country or to buy a particular industrial plant is quite a different task from dealing with repeat decisions by lower level management on routine transactions. The former involves the difficulty of accessing top management and frequently entails a great deal of time spent in providing a wide range of information, hosting visits to the country, and coordinating sales pitches with top government officials, perhaps even the president of the country. In contrast, export promotion usually focuses on purchasing agents or retailers, making sustained presentations unlikely. And deep involvement by other parts of the government is usually not required.

Export promotion has its own special needs. For example, export promotion agencies must often work closely with local firms, to find out what they can deliver, and to assist them in learning how to meet foreigners' standards and scheduling demands. As a result, officials involved in promoting exports must have a thorough understanding of the local business community's capabilities. In contrast, understanding of the capabilities of local businesses and training of local managers plays a relatively minor role in the job of investment promotion.

Similarly, a showroom abroad is important for export promotion, so that local producers can show their wares to potential buyers. Physically displaying products plays little or no role in investment promotion; usually a very small office is adequate. In fact, in CINDE's early efforts in the United States, a room in the home of the promoter stationed near New York served as an adequate base for activity.

Personnel – The Agency Director

Although *Marketing a Country* reported on some of the staffing problems of investment-promotion agencies, it said little about the choice of the director of an agency; a revised version would reflect the importance of this decision to the success of the promotion effort.

The job of directing an investment-promotion agency requires a rare combination of skills. To run a successful organization, the director must communicate regularly and effectively with government officials, maintain political neutrality, and suppress any tendency to flaunt privileges such as higher income or expense accounts associated with entertaining business people. The director must be able to lobby for money—with home and perhaps donor governments—without the support of exact measures of the organization's performance. On the other hand, the director must be able to get along with domestic and foreign business people, fit into their social activities, and perhaps even play golf and tennis. The director must be able to manage a professional organization, where hierarchy is not easily tolerated and where performance of individuals, departments, and the entire organization is not easily measured, with results taking years to assess. The director must also be able to market the success of the organization if funding is to be secured; the director must, at the same time, give credit to others, especially the presiding government. The director must oversee distant offices abroad and supervise routine management tasks such as accounting and budgeting at home and abroad.

Not surprisingly, many managers have not been up to the task. In some cases, where the failure is one of internal management, help can be found in an executive director who takes care of some of the routine management tasks. Still, a number of directors have fallen short. Too often they are political appointees with brief tenures whose ambitions lie in something other than professional investment promotion.

Composition of the Board

The monograph of 10 years ago paid relatively little attention to the structure of boards for investment-promotion agencies. Although the paper did mention them, particularly in connection with the quasi-government structure, the importance of boards necessitates more detailed attention.

Boards can play a role in offsetting the disadvantages associated with particular structures. Thus, agencies that are, by structure, not closely connected with government can alleviate some of the associated problems by including government representatives in their board membership. The presence of government officials can ensure that government is accurately informed of the agency's activities and improve understanding of why the agency's needs, in areas like pay scales, differ from those of the typical government agency. Moreover, government board members provide access to the bureaucracy, which can be extremely valuable when the agency is trying to help investors solve problems with government. Conversely, for the agency that is closely connected with government, a board with members from the private sector offers a compensatory balance. Private sector members are likely to emphasize performance, improve the agency's understanding of how decisions are made in the private sector, and provide information on barriers to investment in the country. The board of the Irish investment promotion agency (IDA) illustrates the effective use of private sector board members.

Problems of Converting from Regulation to Promotion

A very special personnel problem arises when governments attempt to convert a regulatory investment agency into one that focuses on promotion. In fact, it has become conventional wisdom to say that it is very difficult to build effective promotion agencies out of investment agencies whose task in the past was screening investment, accepting or rejecting proposed projects. This point was underemphasized in_Marketing a Country. Presumably, it was less obvious 10 years ago, when the effort to transform old agencies had only a short history. Indeed, the problem has proved greater than most observers realized.

Large, unwieldy organizations whose major function entailed screening investors have had a tendency to remain large and unwieldy, and to remain as barriers to investment from the standpoint of multinational firms. Thus, in June 1999 the national investment agency of Indonesia (BKPM) still had more than 400 employees, required considerable paperwork of investors (although much reduced from its heyday as a control organization), and presented potential investors with an unattractive reception area and poorly prepared information documents. It provided none of the services offered by a number of agencies elsewhere: arranging local appointments, providing car and driver, meeting and assisting arriving investors at the airport, and so on.[7] Many of its staff members remained from the former structure, and they retained an attitude of suspicion of the potential investor.

In 1999, BKPM still had to approve all incoming investment (except for the financial sector and petroleum, which were subject to a different regime).[8] Although the approval process was to be completed within 10 days, investors reported delays as forms were returned to be redone and resubmitted. Although some officials said that approval was virtually automatic, both the questions asked of the investors and internal guidelines in BKPM indicated that negotiations were still being held with investors over technical matters, including proposed production processes, amounts of land required, and locations. Nevertheless, after a decade or more of claiming to be converting, BKPM had shown signs of deemphasizing its control function.

While BKPM called itself a promotion agency, it had only begun to build up its promotion capabilities. In August 1999, less than 10 percent of its professionals were in the foreign investment promotion section, which, instead of a separate division, was still a part of the International Relations Division.

In contrast, the CPI in Mozambique had accomplished complete conversion. Perhaps part of its unusual success came from its being relatively small from the beginning. And normal turnover of personnel meant that by 1999 less than half of its professionals had been with the old-style organization, even though the conversion efforts had begun much more recently than at BKPM. It is also possible that its dependence on World Bank support had been important in the transition. A resident foreign advisor (from the old Dominican Republic agency) had a strong influence on the activities of the CPI. Perhaps also essential to the transition had been the attitude of high-level officials in important ministries. Their desire to dismantle barriers to foreign investment had been manifested in a number of ways, doubtless influencing the orientation of CPI, although it is unlikely that the attitudes alone would have resulted in the conversion. After all, the technocrat ministers in Indonesia had long been unambiguous as to their support of a liberal and open economy and of welcoming policies for foreign investors.

Agencies that have not easily made the transition from license-granting institutions to investment-promotion organizations sometimes seek new ways of holding onto their former power as screening agencies. One may be suspicious that often power is not all that is sought; agencies known for corruption lose a source of income when their licenses are no longer needed. The Indonesian BKPM long sought to reinstitute tax holidays, even though figures on investment after the holidays were abolished in 1984 provide rather persuasive evidence that the holidays had little impact on attracting investors to the country. BKPM also fought hard to retain control over the so-called master list, which exempted approved firms from duties on capital equipment and provided a two-year exemption of raw materials.[9] Although the Thai BOI had a stronger reputation as a promoter of investment, it jealously guarded its somewhat unusual right to grant duty exemptions to investors, even as the economy was liberalized. One wonders whether the EDB in Singapore would be such a staunch supporter of tax incentives if it were not charged with distributing them. It seems that bureaucrats want something of value to give out, even though, as seems the case with the EDB, the reasons are not corruption.

Since conversion from licensing has proved so difficult, some countries have simply begun anew by creating a completely separate organization to carry out investment promotion. This appears to have been the case in Venezuela and Mexico. Given the problems of conversion, this may be the best solution for a number of countries.

Measuring Performance

Marketing a Country contained a chapter entitled "Evaluating the Investment Promotion Function." Yet, many promotion agencies make no attempt to evaluate their performance. Indeed, as pointed out earlier, the difficulty in measuring the performance of an agency is one reason why investment promotion remains a government activity in most countries. If performance were easily measured, the function could probably be contracted out to private enterprise, even though funding would remain a governmental function. Still, even for government agencies, attempts to measure performance can improve management and help it justify funding requests. As imperfect as the measures must be, they are better than no measurements.

In other government activities, when results are difficult to measure, performance is often reported in terms of inputs rather than outputs. In the case of promotion, measurements of efforts include the number of prospective investors visited, expenditures on advertising, number of investment missions undertaken, and similar indices. Results that are possible to measure include estimates of the amount of foreign investment attracted and number of jobs created by firms with which the agency had some contact, even though not all the investments and jobs can be directly attributed to the activities of the agency. Measures of performance can also include results of surveys commissioned by the agency. Surveys cover opinions of the agency held by investors abroad and investors' evaluations of the agency's role in investment decisions (as commissioned by FIAS for CINDE, for example), surveys of recent investors in the country to determine how they evaluate services provided by the agency, and measures of attitude changes from image-building efforts (see reports of evaluations by Investment Canada and the Irish IDA in *Marketing a Country*). Efforts of the private sector to examine the effects of promotional campaigns have generated widely accepted techniques for these kinds of measurement.

Whatever techniques are used, the results will not collapse into a single bottom-line measure of performance in the case of investment promotion agencies. This was not sufficiently emphasized in *Marketing a Country*. As a result of the uncertainty surrounding any feasible measures, evaluations must be presented with some cautions. But, again, they are better than no attempts at evaluation.

Domestic Marketing

Successful promotion agencies have devoted considerable attention not only to marketing their countries abroad but also to marketing themselves at home. The special attention these agencies give to foreigners, the higher salaries some pay to their employees, and the difficulties of attributing investment to their efforts make most agencies easy targets for animosity and budget cuts. As a result, agencies have developed programs that reach out for local support. One common approach is a "linkage program" designed to help domestic firms become suppliers to foreign investors. By showing that foreign firms can be customers, not just competitors, to local business, such programs can generate enthusiasm for foreign investment among domestic business people. Further, successful agencies have produced brochures and other documents that tout their successes. They usually list investors, by name or at least by number of jobs, that they claim to have brought to the country.

Some agencies also carefully point out that their efforts to improve the investment climate for foreign investors benefit local firms as well. They may publicize concrete examples. Moreover, wise promotion agencies probably do not seek incentives for foreign firms that are not available to local firms, since preferences easily create resentment toward both foreign investors and an agency that promotes them.

Some New Policy Issues

Marketing a Country underlines the very successful efforts of certain promotion agencies in attracting foreign investment. Today, observers around the world usually point to the same success stories, particularly the Irish Industrial Development Agency and the Singapore Economic Development Board, who are widely cited as models for other countries. Costa Rica's CINDE is also cited, although its promotion efforts are less visible than those of the two leading agencies. On the other hand, CINDE operates with a budget that is a fraction of the size of the others, and it seems a more realistic model to many countries.

It is almost certainly not an accident that these three promotion agencies are all from small countries and that observers seem to look less often to the promotion agencies of large developing countries as models. This is the case in spite of the fact that some large developing countries, such as China and Indonesia, have attracted very large sums of foreign investment.

It appears that large countries need less of a marketing effort than small countries. As the world's most populous country, China is well known to investors. The potential market of a billion or more people has been enough to bring foreign investors to China without model marketing efforts on the part of the country. Investors came for export projects even when China's domestic market was largely shut off in hopes of someday gaining access to that market. China might benefit from better investment promotion, but promotion is clearly not necessary in order to bring the country to the attention of many investors.

Indonesia, the world's fourth largest country, has been less well known to nonminerals investors, especially those from the United States. On the other hand, as multinational firms more systematically scan the world for potential investment sites, Indonesia has emerged simply because of its size. Moreover, nearby Korean, Japanese, and Taiwan investors—who account for a large part of nonmineral investment in Indonesia—are well aware of the country's domestic market and of the low wage costs that make it a place to manufacture for export. Thus, the usual function of an agency in trying to get the country on the list of places that investors consider is much less important for Indonesia than for smaller countries.

In contrast, Costa Rica, with a population about the size of Greater Boston, was not even well known in the United States as a tourist destination a few years ago. More recently, when Intel sought a new production site, Costa Rica did not appear on the initial list of countries to investigate. In cases like this, promotion is essential. It was the efforts of CINDE that induced Intel to consider (and eventually invest in) Costa Rica.[10]

Although it is more difficult to remember, in the 1960s Singapore was in the Costa Rican category. It was primarily the country's promotion activities that attracted early foreign investors. The success of those investors helped build Singapore's reputation among other investors.

Of course, small countries could, like some large countries, simply ignore foreign investment. On the other hand, the costs of ignoring foreign investment are likely to be higher for small countries than for large ones. Countries like Costa Rica have only a tiny domestic market. If they are to encourage a manufacturing industry, they need access to export markets in order to provide the scale essential for efficiency in most industries. But domestic entrepreneurs are rarely willing to build plants primarily for export markets. When markets are foreign, the risks seem too high. In order to start manufacture for export, some kind of relationship with foreigners is needed; direct foreign investment is usually the most promising.

In sum, especially for small countries, foreign investment is likely to play an important role in efforts to industrialize. However, foreign investment is not likely to go to the small countries unless they undertake promotional efforts. In contrast, large, well-known countries will at least appear on the list of possible investment sites for many potential investors, even if they do little or no promotion. This fact has implications both for the strategy (mix of policies) and the budget of promotion agencies.

Understanding Targeting

Marketing a Country emphasized the need for promotion agencies to target their activities. Many agencies have, nevertheless, found targeting to be a difficult concept. In some cases, agencies fail to consider the motivation of investors when they decide on targets. While they devise lists of the kinds of investors the country wishes to attract, some agencies do not carefully consider whether the investors are likely to have any serious interest in the country.[11] The list of desirable investors can include industries in which investors rarely venture outside of their home countries. Without an understanding of the investor community, targets can be quite unrealistic.

Several agencies have, for example, targeted agriculture, although relatively few firms invest in agriculture abroad. And the firms that do make such investments usually limit their projects to products for which there is a real strategic need for control on the part of the investor. Even plantation agriculture does not attract foreign investment like it once did. Many firms in the industrialized countries are now happy to buy their needs on world markets. Tire companies, for example, at one time owned rubber plantations abroad; they were driven to grow their own rubber as sources fell under the control of competitors, or they were subject to marketing schemes that threatened them with high prices. Since the industry has changed, tire firms now prefer to buy their rubber and most have sold off their plantations. [12] In other plantation activities, foreign firms were active because of the special access they had to capital markets. Hence, the early strength of British and Dutch plantation companies.[13] But this access is no longer so special, and the number of firms interested in such investment has correspondingly shrunk. There are exceptions to the rules, but they are relatively few. A handful of the old British and Dutch plantation firms survive;[14] and foreign firms do still grow bananas, for example; but for reasons special to the product.

On the other hand, foreign firms are more often interested in agricultural *processing* industries. Foreign firms will, for example, build canneries for tomatoes, although they are unlikely to invest in growing them. Nevertheless, they are willing to provide technical help to local growers, including, sometimes, financing. Understanding industry structure and changes such as these can turn impractical targeting into useful targeting.

Targeting was described in *Marketing a Country* as defining focus in terms of industry, size of country, and firm characteristics (usually size). Yet, some other criteria have emerged in recent efforts at targeting. Most conspicuous have been targets based on ethnic identity. Thus, Croatia has identified as a target the Croat diaspora, especially in North America, Australia, and Chile. India has reportedly recently begun to target people of Indian descent abroad.[15] Significant successes in these efforts to reach particular ethnic groups have not been reported, but it may be that the attempts are too recent to have produced notable results.[16]

On occasion, countries overlook advantages that they hold and which can be important to foreign investors. Mauritius successfully attracted foreign investors more than a decade ago based on its preferential access to the European Union, as an ACP country. Yet, a number of other ACP countries have failed to promote the similar advantages they offer. Countries that benefit from other trade arrangements have also failed to exploit them. For example, it recently proved difficult for FIAS consultants to get a clear statement within CINDE about the status of Costa Rican products with regard to tariff preferences in the United States. The agency was clearly not using preferences as a means of identifying investors who might develop an interest in Costa Rica.

Moreover, surprisingly little is done by most promotion agencies to monitor investment in their own and in other similar countries. Investors who seek out a country on their own provide strong clues as to which other investors are prospects; if one investor in a particular activity comes, there are likely to be other firms with similar characteristics who are prospective investors. Other countries also provide hints for building target lists. Ireland watches investment flows elsewhere, but few agencies in developing countries seek lists of investors in other countries to help in identifying target industries or individual firms to go after. The failure to use information about investors in an agency's own and other countries constitutes a serious omission on the part of many promotion agencies.

Sometimes investment-promotion agencies carry targeting too far. They prepare informational and promotional material only for the industries they have named as targets. If prospective investors appear from sectors outside the target list, they do not have appropriate informational material to offer. Some agencies, CINDE said to be one, have shown a tendency to pass such prospects on to other government entities.

Targeting should govern activities where the agency has to initiate action. Thus, targeting is important for advertising, for designing promotional seminars, and for identifying firms on which representatives will call. It should not, however, limit the efforts of a promotion agency to help prospective investors who take the initiative, whether they are on the target list or not.

Subnational Investment-Promotion Agencies

Marketing a Country did not explore the role of subnational promotion agencies, although it did include some such agencies in its sample. Subnational agencies can be quite independent of each other and of any national agency, such as those in the United States, for example. In other cases, they are little more than branch offices of a national organization. The Thai BOI has offices in various regions of Thailand, which are branches of the BOI itself. The BKPM similarly has offices in various parts of Indonesia. In still other cases, such as China and Vietnam, the relationships between local offices and national offices seem quite ambiguous to an outsider.

The performance of subnational offices is worthy of additional study. Some appear to be quite effective, in a few cases even more effective than national offices. On the contrary, in other countries local agencies seem to be barriers to rather than promoters of investment.

The differences across countries seemingly cannot be explained simply by whether the local agencies are branches or independent; however, on average, independent agencies may perform better. Some of the differences, at least within the branch category, appear to result from the characteristics of the government of the country in question. In highly centralized countries such as Indonesia, local agencies seem not to respond strongly to local interests. This may be the result of career patterns. Officials see their careers as being advanced within the national system, not by building a local constituency. Perhaps, as a result, many of the local BKPM offices are not driven by local interests in attracting investment. In this case, local offices have a reputation of collecting rents from investors rather than encouraging them. On the other hand, in more decentralized countries, local officials seem to respond more to local economic interests. Thus, in China local government officials see their promotion routes largely within the region, or, if within the central government, as being based on furthering the regional economy. There, promotion agencies are likely to respond to local needs and, consequently, compete with each other for investment. But, these are no more than untested hypotheses.

Understanding regional offices is important. It seems, for example, that they can, under certain circumstances, be very effective voices for policy reform. Moreover, they may turn out to be useful in reducing corruption and bureaucratic red tape. In other government functions, competition within the government has proved useful for accomplishing similar goals. In Indonesia, for example, competition among the different organizations that run the duty drawback and exemption system, the export processing zones, and bonded factories appears to have limited the corruption and red tape facing exporters. If one of these organizations raises too many investment barriers for exporters, firms can go to another, leaving the problem organization with fewer clients. It may be that the current experiment in investment licensing in Indonesia will have similar results. In 1999, BKPM began to allow regional investment offices (and some foreign embassies) to issue investment licenses in the hope that the process would be accelerated and become more investor friendly. Whether this experiment works in a competitive way will depend on the response of local investment authorities.

Opportunities for Collaboration

In the research for *Marketing a Country*, we did not encounter investment-promotion agencies that had attempted to coordinate their activities with agencies of other countries[17] or which had tried to encourage movement of investors in their country to other countries. Cooperation seemed to be limited to the efforts of some agencies to provide assistance to agencies in poorer countries. The Irish IDA, for example, had loaned an official to Costa Rica's CINDE to help it develop its programs. And, at the time of the study or soon thereafter, the Thai BOI began to assist the Lao PDR investment authority. While this kind of assistance has increased and has proved very helpful to new agencies, other kinds of cooperative efforts have developed. The Investment Promotion Network (IPAnet) has, for instance, provided a vehicle for exchange of information.

Of interest as well have been the overseas activities of the Singapore EDB and its affiliates. As mentioned, the agency, through an affiliate, established industrial estates on Batam Island in Indonesia and in Johore Baru in Malaysia, and encouraged manufacturing firms that faced high wages in Singapore to locate their manufacturing facilities in these nearby sites where wages were lower. The EDB hoped that relocation to Batam Island or to Johore Baru would lead firms to keep headquarters, financial operations, service, and distribution in Singapore. By operating industrial estates in neighboring countries, EDB provided a certain degree of security to firms that were accustomed to Singapore efficiency and freedom from corruption.[18] In Indonesia, for example, Singaporean management promised to handle all the government formalities for firms located in the zone it ran. If "unofficial" payments were required, the private foreign firm would not have to be involved. By 1995, Singapore was considering other "growth triangles" in nearby countries, including a zone north of Medan in Sumatra.[19]

Possibilities in other countries for efforts similar to the EDB model are likely to appear. Success in building foreign investment has meant rising wages. As a result, some of the early investors in very labor-intensive and cost-sensitive industries have to relocate after a time. Where neighboring countries provide possible sites, it may be in the interest of the country losing the plant to assist in the process and try to retain some of the high-wage jobs. Textile firms in Costa Rica, for example, began to relocate to Honduras and Nicaragua when Costa Rican labor became too expensive and as these neighboring countries opened for investment. There may be gains for Costa Rica, an attractive place for executives, in recognizing the inevitability of the transition and in thus trying to influence how it occurs. As mentioned, in 1999 it appeared that the investment agency of Mauritius recognized similar possibilities and was discussing the prospects of cooperating with the development of export processing zones in lower wage Mozambique (and perhaps elsewhere).

By 1999, other proposals for cooperation among investment-promotion agencies had been floated. A grand study commissioned by the Inter-American Development Bank to examine prospects for Central American countries had proposed joint promotion efforts for the region.[20] By the summer of 1999, the details had not been explained in any publicly available document, however. Similarly, a proposal had been circulated for the sharing of image-building efforts by some reform-minded African countries.[21] Another cooperation effort had been initiated by countries along the Mekong River.[22] Although the interests of neighboring investment-promotion agencies are likely to conflict with each other when investment-generation activities are involved, it is possible that there may be joint gains in cooperating in image-building activities, if the countries have undertaken similar reforms. Image building is especially expensive. For small countries, experiments in joint image building might turn out to be valuable.

A Final Note

The basic premises of *Marketing a Country* have stood the test of a decade, but more has been learned in the intervening years.. Investment promotion is a constantly evolving field. Investment-promotion agencies continue to experiment; some experiments succeed, and many fail. But all offer lessons to others. Additionally, promotion activities seem to be growing outside the bounds of the narrowly defined investment- promotion agency. And, like business, a few of the agencies are becoming international, directly or through alliances. Ten years from now there will surely be a great deal more to write on investment promotion.

Notes

1. Louis T. Wells and Alvin Wint, *Marketing a Country: Promotion as a Tool for Attracting Foreign Investment* (Washington, D.C.: FIAS, 1990).

2. For a write-up of this effort, see Timothy Buehrer and Louis T. Wells, *Cutting Red Tape: Lessons from a Case-based Approach to Improving the Investment Climate in Mozambique* (tentative title, forthcoming from FIAS).

3. An important exception occurs when a firm controls land for industrial estates or export processing zones. This situation is covered later in this paper.

4. *Strengthening Investment Promotion Agencies: The Role of the Private Sector* (Washington, D.C.: FIAS, March 1999, unpublished).

5. Ibid.

6. From interviews conducted by the authors in the early 1990s.

7. It claimed to provide such services, calling on the Department of Tourism, which was under the same minister. But there was little evidence of implementation of the "welcoming" program.

8. In July 1999 the *Jakarta Post* announced a change that would allow local BKPMs to approve investment. The implementing decrees had, however, not yet been issued. See "Investment Licensing Powers to be Delegated to Provinces," *Jakarta Post*, July 21, 1999.

9. As of August 1999 BKPM had retained control of the master list for new investment, but lost it to Customs for expansions.

10. The story is documented in Debora Spar, *Attracting High Technology Investment: Intel's Costa Rican Plant* (Washington, D.C.: FIAS, 1998).

11. In the manufacturing sectors, some of the especially unrealistic targeting occurs in former communist countries, whose grasp of Western

firms is shaky. A recent document from the Slovak Republic, for example, exemplified a focus based on desires, with little thought to the interests of investors. SNAZIR, "Slovak Government Strategy to Support Foreign Direct Investment," Bratislava, April 1999.

12. Partial substitution of synthetic rubber probably played some role in the change as well. See Mira Wilkins and Harm Schroeter, *The Free Standing Company in the World Economy, 1830–1996*. Oxford: Oxford University Press, 1998.

13. Ibid.

14. These firms have not always retained their original nationalities. Some British plantation firms have, for example, been bought by Malaysians.

15. See Celia W. Dugger, "India Offers Rights to Attract Its Offspring's Cash," *New York Times*, April 4, 1999, p. 4.

16. On the other hand, the importance of ethnic ties in foreign investment decisions is emphasized in one of the earliest studies of how firms make locational decisions. See Yair Aharoni, *The Foreign Investment Decision Process* (Boston: Division of Research, Harvard Business School, 1966).

17. There were some examples of rent sharing, encouraged by UNIDO, through common space in high-rent areas such as New York City.

18. The program of establishing overseas estates was not limited to these two countries, but the motivations for some of the others appear to be somewhat different.

19. Singapore had also become involved in industrial estates in China and India, partly in response to the ethnic mix of Singaporeans.

20. The study was led by Jeff Sachs and Michael Porter.

21. Louis T. Wells, "Marketing a Region for Trade and Investment" in *Africa and the American Private Sector: Corporate Perspective on a Growing Relationship*. Washington, D.C.: The Corporate Council on Africa, 1977), pp. 88–88.

22. For a description, see http://www.adb.org/Work/GMS/invest_tor.asp.